English Cocker Spaniel Training

English Cocker Spaniel Training includes: English Cocker Spaniel Tricks, Socializing, Housetraining, Agility, Obedience, Behavioral Training, and More

---

Joe Peters

ISBN 978-1-5269-1137-7

A Great Thanks

I would like to start by thanking the many wonderful English Cocker Spaniel breeders in existence today. Through your hard work and dedication, we are fortunate enough to experience the many joys that come with owning and training this great breed.

Thank you to my publishers that have allowed for this book to become a reality.

A Great Thank You to my family for their loving support during this project.

Table of Contents

Foreword

As a family, we have had the pleasure of owning and training a series of dogs and puppies over the last 40 years. The experience, the satisfaction, the delights and joys that I have encountered is what has led me to share what I have learnt with you.

This training guide is intended for English Cocker Spaniel owners. On the whole, I found the English Cocker Spaniel to respond well to training and particularly to positive rewards-based training like the systems covered in this book.

The day that your new English Cocker Spaniel arrives is one filled with excitement and joy. The future feels bright and full of a lot of imagined good times.

This can all turn very quickly into frustration if your daily walks become an episode of yanking and yelling, or if your English Cocker Spaniel just won't follow your cues.

However, it doesn't have to be this way. Unfortunately not all owners have a good experience with training their companion, and can tend to opt for aggressive punishment based techniques. This, coupled with a lack of confidence, has led to many owners being put off from training and just finding their own way while putting up with bad canine behavior as their way of life.

With training, your companionship bond will be nurtured, and it can be truly satisfying and successful while being enjoyable for both you and your English Cocker Spaniel. Stick with it and your efforts will pay off.

1st Chapter: Introduction

The mutualistic symbiotic relationship between humans and dogs has been found to extend back for more than 30,000 years. Perhaps continuing research will push this date back even further – speculation based on findings in caves has placed a date of up to 300,000 years ago on the beginning of the dog/ human partnership. Our relationship with dogs has proved to be beneficial for both species on several levels, including the emotional, which demonstrates that our dependence upon one another goes past a mere physical need.

It is quite easy to imagine how our relationship with dogs began, when humans were living around so many large and dangerous beasts. During the Paleolithic era, when most scientists agree that we and dogs got together, humans not only had to contend with large, dangerous herbivores like mammoths, wooly rhinoceros, and aurochs, but also with animals that preyed directly on them such as cave lions, wolves, and cave bears. Dogs would have provided not only some protection against these predators, especially in union with their humans, but also as an early warning system.

Flying in the face of conventional thinking is the possibility that our domestic dogs did not evolve from wolves. However, there are some very convincing arguments to be made that dogs developed from a now extinct canine form. Wolves can be considered to be impossible to truly tame or train. During the Middle Ages, a concerted effort was made by the hunting nobility in Europe to domesticate the wolf since it was stronger and hardier than any of the dogs, even mastiffs, that were used for hunting big game. The effort was a total failure; basically, although wolf puppies will seem to tame and become attached to humans, once they reach sexual maturity, they revert to a wild 'frame of mind'. The same happens with nearly every other wild animal that humans have raised; once the animal reaches puberty it becomes unreliable. Male wolves kept in a captive state, even if familiar with the keeper, will attack the keeper if he or she comes between him and a female in estrus.

Our ancestors, dealing with challenging environmental conditions, would not have had much to do with a large predator like the wolf, which preyed on human beings. Humans of the time would have seen the wolf as a competitor or threat.

Wolves still attack and even kill human beings today, after centuries of decimation of the animals has left the most timid wolves in the gene pool. How much bolder, and more ferocious those early wolves must have been – humans have never domesticated tigers for much the same reasons; the animals are powerful killers, not animals content to beg for scraps from raggle-taggle early humans. It may be much more likely that a smallish, now extinct dog that came slinking to a campfire for scraps, rolling onto its back to present its belly, is a much more likely candidate for domestication than the ferocious wolf. These smaller canids would have to have shown themselves to be amenable to training fairly quickly, otherwise they probably would have ended up being roasted on a spit.

The Fox Experiment

A very interesting experiment was conducted by Dmitry Belyaev, who was a Soviet geneticist. Using silver foxes, Belyaev instituted a breeding program that was supposed to show how selective breeding could turn a wild animal, such as a wolf, into a domestic dog. Over a span of 40+ years, Belyaev and his assistants chose the most amenable and least fearful kits from litters of silver foxes and bred them together. At the time of Belyaev's death in 1985, the experiment had only progressed for 26 years, and has continued until recently. As time passed, the researchers found that both the physical and mental characteristics of the foxes changed – they started barking, they showed variation in size, and their coat color, length, and texture changed. The ears of the foxes became floppy. Most significantly, a proportion of the former foxes sought the company of humans, wagging their tails and whining to attract attention.

While this monumental study, which actually used something like 35,000 foxes over the course of the experiment, does show that it is possible to transform semi-tame foxes from fur farms into dogs, it also illustrates something else – the sheer impossibility of early humans, struggling to survive in a hostile and incredibly dangerous world, to manipulate by selective breeding a vicious and unpredictable predator like the wolf to become their tame and friendly companions. How on earth could people who lived on the edge of starvation and predation themselves, often in a nomadic lifestyle as they followed the herds on their migrations, have devoted the time and energy and foresight needed to transform wolves into dogs. Doesn't it make more sense to suppose that dogs something like the pariah dogs of today are the ancestors of the dogs that share our lives currently? The sheer logistics of the fox project, which even began with semi-tame foxes, would certainly be beyond the scope of Cro-Magnon, or Early Modern Human, mankind.

DNA studies are often touted as 'proving' that dogs evolved from wolves, but actually prove little more than that over the eons some dogs have been bred to wolves. Huskies and sled dogs are routinely bred to wolves from time to time to increase their hardihood, while the so-called 'timber shepherds' are hybrids resulting from crossing a German Shepherd (usually), with a wolf. Keep in mind that DNA testing is not the most exact science; in most testing procedures, the DNA from two animals, say a wolf and a German Shepherd, is mixed together, then allowed to settle out. The degree of relatedness is then determined by how many pieces of the wolf chromosome come together with the German Shepherd chromosome. This probably works in a general way. Keep in mind, too, that the Pekingese is thought to be one of the dogs closest to the wolf, something which the morphology of the Pekingese screams against.

Divorcing wolves from dogs is important as far as dog training is concerned because many theories about dog behavior and training are based on the social structure of a wolf pack. It would perhaps be better to examine the behavior of pariah dogs or feral dogs to get a closer approximation of the behavior of the real ancestors of today's dogs.

Pack Behavior in Wild and Feral Canids

Undoubtedly, the behavior of wolves in a wild state has been one of the most studied. Researchers have, up until fairly recently, considered that wolf packs were groups of perhaps partially-related and non-related individuals kept in line by an 'alpha' male and female. Studies of wild wolves have shown that wolf 'packs' are actually family groups, with the parent wolves being, of course, the leaders, and the younger wolves their variously aged offspring. Most wolf packs only contain 5 to 7 members, although pack size is in direct proportion to the availability of prey animals.

The younger wolves eventually leave the pack when they are 2 to 3 years old to find mates with which to begin their own family group, but before they branch off, they do help to care for their younger siblings as well as participating in hunts. There is dominance behavior shown to the younger family members by the parents, but constant jockeying for the top position is not part of the family structure.

African hunting dogs show some similarities with wolf family groups, but there are some important differences. While African hunting dog social structure is based generally on a family group, these groups are usually larger than that displayed by wolves, and groups will often combine when herbivores are migrating to take advantage of the large amount of prey. As with wolves, hunting dogs have only one breeding pair in the group, but it seems that males in the group can move up to occupy the top position by fighting. Older, displaced males are usually allowed to remain in the pack. Only the younger female hunting dogs leave the pack to join other groups – male offspring or 'adoptees' do not.

Jackals and coyotes show very similar breeding and social behavior in their respective niches. In both cases, as is that with wolves, young of these species stay with the parents for several years before leaving to establish their own families. During this time, they help with care of the new young and learn the refinements of hunting and scavenging.

And, although most people think of foxes as being entirely solitary animals except for the mother and her kits, this species does exhibit a family structure very much like that of other wild canids. The parent foxes establish a hunting territory, like wolves, coyotes, and jackals, and use this as a base in which to raise their young. The young from the previous year often do remain with the parents for a time to assist with raising the new litter. If the chances seem good, it is likely that non-breeding individuals will leave to establish their own territories, but the young will stay with the parents for an extended period should there be little opportunity for them.

The family, or pack, structure of all of the above animals is very similar, and another similarity they have is that the dominant pair is monogamous. This differs greatly from the social life that is observed in pariah (feral) dogs. Pariah dogs do not form family packs at all; dogs that are unattached to humans follow the same pattern around the world – they may come together briefly to exploit a food resource, or when a female is in heat, but there is no cohesive structure, and the 'pack' evaporates as soon as the control is removed. Feral female dogs will mate with any number of males, unlike the wild canids where the female mates with only one male dog.

In another respect, feral dogs show none of the family structure present in wolves, jackals, or foxes. The mother dog has sole responsibility for raising the litter of pups – the father takes no part. Young dogs soon leave their mothers to live a semi-solitary existence. Feral dogs will 'hang around' in the same general area, but have yet to show any real tendency to fight for an alpha position.

There is another interesting side to the supposition that dogs evolved from wolves, and that is that when once domesticated animals become feral, after several generations they revert to the original type. In other words, if a flock of chickens escaped confinement and were able to survive and breed away from human intervention, they would come to more closely resemble the red jungle fowl which is their distant ancestor. With regards to dogs that become separated from active association with humans, feral dogs revert to the basic pariah dog model – they do not become wolves.

Training Theories Based on Pack Behavior

A great many of today's dog training strategies are based on early observations of a captive wolf pack. These were wolves that were basically thrown indiscriminately together in a zoo in Switzerland. Unlike natural wolf packs, based on family structure and hierarchy, these wolves were strangers to one another, and denied of any opportunity to disperse, had little alternative than to fight with one another. In a wolf family, there is a dominance hierarchy, with the father and mother wolves at the top; it's only natural that even in an artificial situation, the instinctive drive for a normal 'pack' structure would surface, although in a completely distorted manner.

Most dog training programs have been based on these early, flawed descriptions of wolf pack behavior. These training programs generally call for the dog owner to exert his or her authority over the dog at all times, but especially when training the animal. Letting your dog walk in front of you or eat before you do were thought to undermine your authority as the pack leader. These theories do have some basis in reality if the wolf pack model is followed – the parent wolves do maintain their authority over the younger wolves, and will discipline them if their behavior violates the established behavior. Adult wolves will attack their older offspring for attempting to mate with one another or with the parents. Tempers appear to become shorter the closer it comes to the time when the young wolves would normally leave the family group.

It seems very probable, that if one accepts at least the possibility that domestic dogs evolved from a small to medium scavenging canine that hung around humans, that the wolf pack model is wrong to either a greater or lesser extent. Humans and dogs have interacted for so many thousands of years, and have developed so many intricacies of behavior with one another that training based strictly on forming dominance over the dog is probably incorrect. Experiments with tame wolves and dogs have shown over and over that dogs will turn to their humans for help when presented with a task beyond their means, whereas the wolves will struggle on (to reach food, for instance) even if there is no way for them to attain their goal by themselves.

Yes, obviously dogs must be subordinate to the humans, but the object of training should never be to break the dog's spirit, but to help the dog form a stronger relationship with the human family, one that is based more on trust and respect than aggression and fear.

Why Training Works – Human/Dog Mutualism

There are considered to be three symbiotic relationships in nature: parasitism, commensalism, and mutualism. Parasitism is well understood by nearly everyone and involves one species benefitting at the expense of another; internal parasites such as roundworms or liver flukes come to mind, as well as external parasites such as ticks and fleas. Commensalism is a symbiotic condition where one of the partners will benefit, and while the other receives no harm, it likewise receives no benefit; air plants (epiphytes) such as orchids and bromeliads, attach themselves to the trunks and limbs of trees, lessening the chances of predation by plant eaters and exposing them to more sunlight than they would have received on the forest floor, and cattle egret follow herds of cattle to eat the insects that the cattle inadvertently disturb – in both of these cases, the host tree or the cow receives no benefit, but neither is it hurt in any way.

The relationship between dogs and humans, however, is probably one of the best examples of mutualism. Over the thousands of years of our association with dogs, our mutual dependence upon the other species has actually changed both physiologically as well as psychologically. Humans and dogs have grown so close that our genes have come to mirror each other in certain important areas: digestion, brain functions, diet, and diseases. In fact, some researchers have conducted tests to demonstrate that the reactions of dogs to different stimuli create identical brain waves to those produced by human beings. Dogs are the only animals that look at both sides of our faces when interacting with us, and they learn to smile by watching us; they are intelligent enough to pick up on the emotions that accompany smiling and use their smiles appropriately.

Dogs have been found, by using brain scans, to share the same set of emotions that their owners do. These were things that those who are close to dogs knew already, but now science has proven this. The areas of the brain dealing with emotions such as joy, love, or jealousy match those of humans, and dogs react in the same way, with the same brain waves, as do their owners when these emotions are stimulated. Dogs are considered to have the intelligence of a human toddler, and it is only their inability to actually speak that stands in the way of what might be considered a more perfect bonding with humans.

However, it is precisely this mutualistic relationship that lends itself so well to training dogs. Not only are dogs highly intelligent, they also 'think' like we do. Over the course of human/dog evolution, dogs have been shaped to fulfill different needs – hunting, guarding, active protection, herding, and simply as companions. The trainability of dogs depends not only on their breed, but also upon the individual. Dogs of a certain breed, gun dogs or herding dogs, for example, are generally easy to train as they have worked in tandem with their owners to achieve a certain goal.

In my experience, English Cocker Spaniels are not the most difficult of dogs to train, however a key determining factor in successful training lies within the individual owner's experience and variations of applied approach.

Guard dogs tend to be more independent minded as they evolved to provide guarding for flocks or even villages without humans being present at all times. Some were expected to be able to make decisions on their own, and while this was obviously a useful trait while guarding a flock of sheep in an isolated situation on the Central Anatolian Plateau, it can cause training difficulties. However, always keep in mind that most problems concerning training can be overcome by using the correct technique and approach.

Training your English Cocker Spaniel requires patience, technique, and an understanding and acceptance of the characteristics of your dog's breed. Properly training your dog will not only help to establish the dog's position in the family, but will help to establish a stronger bond between owner and pet.

2nd Chapter: Socializing Your English Cocker Spaniel

The need for active socialization will vary from breed to breed, depending on breed characteristics, but even a good-natured companion dog like an English Cocker Spaniel will benefit from being socialized. Unless the breeder from whom you purchase your English Cocker Spaniel has taken an extremely active part in raising your puppy, you may find that your new English Cocker Spaniel is a bit shy and perhaps apprehensive around people and other pets. This may be perfectly normal, but an English Cocker Spaniel who is never socialized will probably never be the confident and self-assured dog it should be.

Years ago, when I helped to raise a litter of puppies, I made it a point to handle them every day, right from birth. Because the mother was incapable of caring for them, I cleaned them and helped them feed, even providing supplemental feedings when one of them started to lose weight. Now, even though they were used to my smell and the touch of my hands, when their eyes opened, and they saw how huge I was in comparison, they were actually afraid of me. I was able to overcome this fairly quickly, but imagine how a puppy who has never had this kind of treatment must feel when they first enter a new home – it must be very frightening to them. My puppies had no problems whatsoever with meeting new people and all of them adjusted to their new homes without any problem at all; basically, they came pre-socialized in a way.

However, you should keep something in mind before you take your English Cocker Spaniel puppy around to different situations to help socialize it – your pup should have had its required vaccinations. Many canine diseases are easily transmittable (such as distemper, parvovirus, and coronavirus) and are usually more serious in young dogs than they will be in older ones. Puppies do receive some immunity from their mother's milk, but this will wear off quickly and leave your English Cocker Spaniel exposed to various bacterial and viral diseases.

The first dogs your English Cocker Spaniel should meet should be those of friends or relatives that are calm and friendly animals. Don't hesitate to ask whether the dogs have been vaccinated themselves, as inoculations are not 100% effective. You can even arrange to have your English Cocker Spaniel puppy meet the other dogs on 'neutral ground', such as during a walk. Stay positive and praise your pup when it responds favorably to the meeting.

English Cocker Spaniels, like all dogs, have psychological windows during which receptivity to new experiences will be most likely to be positive. When your English Cocker Spaniel puppy is around 12 to 14 weeks old, this is the perfect age to begin socialization. Once again, pay attention to vaccinations before embarking on this. This is also the perfect time for you to begin using very mild forms of discipline with your puppy. By mild forms of discipline, I mean telling the puppy "No" in a fairly stern voice. It does not mean striking the puppy in any way or confining it to a crate to punish it. Relying mostly on positive reinforcement with occasional verbal reprimands will actually make your pup more confident because it will realize that it can depend on you to take care of it. Even an English Cocker Spaniel will try to move to the dominant position in a home if there seems to be no leadership available, but dogs seem to understand that they are not really competent to act as the alpha in the household and will actually appreciate it when you show yourself to be the leader. You, your family, and your English Cocker Spaniel will be all the happier if you attend to this facet of socialization.

Besides allowing your English Cocker Spaniel to meet other dogs and people, it's a good idea to take it to different situations such as parks, streets in towns or cities, other people's homes, stores that may allow dogs inside, etc. This allows your English Cocker Spaniel puppy to become accustomed to noise and movement, so it will be less likely to be fearful or panic in the future.

Always remember to keep your English Cocker Spaniel on a leash when outside the home. Some owners choose to use a harness instead of a collar. You may find that a harness is better for control. It will also be more comfortable for your English Cocker Spaniel since no pressure will be placed on the throat.

Enrolling your English Cocker Spaniel puppy in puppy obedience classes is also a good way to socialize it. Not only will it allow your pup to interact with other young dogs and their owners, but it will help with discipline in a positive manner. English Cocker Spaniels that have exhibited shyness can often get over it by attending puppy obedience classes. Not only will your English Cocker Spaniel learn how to behave, but you will also be taught how to effectively train your pup. Make certain the operator of the class has certification and experience, and it's best to speak to them beforehand to get an idea of their methods. If you have no idea where to find a puppy obedience class, ask your veterinarian for a recommendation.

3rd Chapter: Housetraining English Cocker Spaniel Puppies and Adults

Using the house or apartment as a bathroom is probably one of the greatest reasons, other than aggression, why dogs wind up in animal shelters. Housetraining is often looked upon as being one of the major hurdles that an English Cocker Spaniel puppy or adult must overcome before being completely accepted as a member of the family. The time and effort that it takes to housetrain a puppy, or even an adult, can be extensive, so patience, as well as consistency, is required. If you react with anger, screaming, and striking the animal, it will only have a negative effect and can cause long-term psychological problems with your pet, as well as not advancing the project one jot.

In most cases, English Cocker Spaniel puppies will be acquired from a kennel. Kennels handle the housing of dogs much differently than ordinary pet owners who might occasionally produce a litter of pups. Dogs in kennels, and litters of pups, are kept in fairly small enclosures, sometimes with no opportunity to go outside at all. One of the adult dogs we got from a kennel had never been out of her cage at all, and she actually had trouble walking; she would trip over a twig on the ground, literally. Slowly, she learned how to walk normally and run, and did she love to stretch out her length once she figured out how to do it, it was pure joy for her. These animals never have the opportunity to learn how to use the outdoors for elimination, and must use their living space when they urinate or defecate. English Cocker Spaniel puppies from kennels or puppy mills, and adult dogs adopted from them, are starting at ground zero in regards to housetraining, and must be taught the proper elimination behavior.

Interestingly, when we had a litter of English Cocker Spaniel puppies years ago, they were given the run of the house along with their parents. To begin with, of course, they simply went to the bathroom wherever the urge took them, and we just cleaned the messes up without comment. However, they observed their mother and father going outside to do their business, and at 6 weeks, one of the puppies started going to the door, asking to go out; it was truly an incredible sight to see that tiny puppy standing at the door, waiting to be let outside. We also worked with all the puppies to at least begin housetraining. When these 4 pups were adopted by other people, none of them eliminated in their new homes even once, not even to mark territory; all of them instantly went outside, even using doggy doors after being shown. From this, it's hard to escape the conclusion that even very young puppies are capable of being housetrained fairly easily as long as they have the example of older dogs and a little help from their human friends.

When we brought our last English Cocker Spaniel puppies home, we allowed them to sleep in our bed right from the start. They spent their first night snuggled next to us. There was no whining or crying, and they settled down and went to sleep without a fuss. They got up once during the night to urinate, and never soiled the bed either.

We humans should keep in mind that up until the time that puppies join their new family, they are accustomed to sleeping with their mother and siblings; they are warm and in constant physical contact with others, which makes them feel secure, and we mirrored this as much as possible with our pups. Within 2 weeks these 3 month old puppies were sleeping through the night, and they still maintain this schedule after 11 years.

Unrealistic Expectations

Obviously, there are very few people who appreciate finding their rug soaked with urine or dog feces on the floor. And, unfortunately, many people react with anger when they find an unwanted 'deposit'. Housetraining takes a great deal of work, especially with English Cocker Spaniel puppies, and if you're looking for a 5 day miracle, you are going to be sadly disappointed. Thinking that you can housetrain a puppy in under a week is analogous to thinking that a human child of 8 months can be taken out of diapers – it just can't be done.

Housetraining a puppy will require weeks of fairly intensive interaction with the pup, and this can be especially difficult if the pup will be left alone for long hours while you are at work. It is, naturally, easiest to housetrain your pet if you are there throughout the day to monitor the pup, but it can be achieved even if you are out of the home during the day.

You will become far less frustrated and irritated if you take the whole process slowly and methodically, and keep a fairly philosophical outlook such as 'this too shall pass'. Puppies and dogs don't want to soil their home, and are not doing this to get back at you in any way.

There are a series of dog breeds that appear to have their own schedule in regards to housetraining with some breeds being much easier to train than others. There are, however, plenty of breeds that may present more of a housebreaking challenge to the owner.

Smaller dogs in general are considered to be more difficult to housetrain than larger dogs, and owners of such should be prepared to be patient with their dog. The most difficult pup or adult dog to housebreak will nearly always be trained if enough time and patience is invested in the project. As far as housetraining goes, there is absolutely no place for negative reinforcement in the process. Praise should be used for success, and failures should be completely ignored.

With your English Cocker Spaniel, be sure to display absolute patience at every step of the process. English Cocker Spaniels, like most dogs, are very sensitive to the reactions of their owners.

Starting Sensibly with Your English Cocker Spaniel Puppy

The first thing to understand is that the gastrointestinal system and urinary system are still in a developmental stage in a puppy that is only a couple of months old. When puppies are born, they require the assistance of the mother to go to the bathroom, she licks their bottoms to stimulate them to urinate and defecate. This is obviously a strategy to keep the den clean. Once they start moving about a bit on their own, pups will still have no ability to hold urine or feces for some weeks to come and will soil indiscriminately; their mother still cleans up after them at this point.

Consider that an English Cocker Spaniel puppy younger than 12 weeks will be unable to control its bowel and bladder functions, you may luck out like we did with our 6 week old puppy, but in most cases, you will be dealing with a puppy that has no idea of where to eliminate. There are several reasons why this occurs, and it should never be considered that the puppy is being disobedient:

1. The bladder of a puppy, especially of the smaller breeds, is relatively tiny. As time goes on, it will stretch out and expand, but initially it is little more than a tube. There would be no way that a puppy could 'hold it' at this early point.

2. The sphincter muscles of the bladder and colon are not developed in a very young dog so are unable to exert any control.

3. In order for a puppy to be able to control itself, the neural connections between the brain, bladder, and colon must be completed, and this will proceed as nature has provided; there is no way that this can be hurried along.

Expecting too much from your English Cocker Spaniel puppy to begin with is a perfect recipe for frustration and anger on your part and fear on that of the puppy. Results will occur much more quickly and reliably when the owner is patient and avoids negativity of any kind.

Probably the most important facet of housetraining is to get the puppy onto a schedule as quickly as possible. You should feed the puppy at the same times every day, and the pup should go to bed at the same time every night. Establishing a routine is essential for helping your puppy learn how and when to use papers or the outdoors for elimination. You can start this as soon as you get your puppy, even if it is too young to actually be housetrained. This is also a good way just to help the pup feel more confident in regards to the new family and situation.

Take the puppy out every hour during the day, if possible, to help establish this as a routine too. You will be able to gradually lengthen the time between trips as the puppy gets older. Either forego outside trips or make them very brief if the weather is beastly, as this can act as an unintentional negative reinforcement too. Short-haired puppies will be very uncomfortable during cold or rainy weather and will often resist going outside because of this; sometimes a coat or sweater can help.

However you start housetraining your puppy, never, ever yell at your puppy, strike it, or rub its nose in the mess. Even telling the pup "No!" in a loud voice is totally unnecessary, this is not a discipline problem, it is a biological barrier to be overcome. Not only is this only providing negative reinforcement, some of these reactions are cruel and will only serve to make your pup afraid of you.

Paper Training

There are a number of reasons why you may want to start housetraining your English Cocker Spaniel puppy with paper training: you live in an apartment and getting the puppy outside quickly could be difficult, the winter weather is so extreme that you hesitate to expose a very young puppy to it, and you are not present in the home during part of the day. The point of paper training is to get the puppy used to going to the bathroom in one or two spots, rather than anywhere the urge takes the pup. This will probably require quite a few newspapers, so it's a good idea to start stocking up before you even bring your puppy home. Some people prefer to use 'training pads' for this rather than newspaper, and these do have the advantage of having plastic on the bottom to prevent leakage.

Simply expect your new puppy to urinate and defecate on the floor, and this is actually the first step to paper training. You should just take this in stride; don't make any kind of fuss over this, either positive or negative. Your puppy will naturally be attracted to where urine or feces have been previously, so use some of these substances to train your puppy.

1. Place the paper you will be using near your exit or exits if possible, this will help the puppy to learn to associate elimination with going outside in time. One of our females still goes over to one of the places where she was taught to use newspapers when she was a puppy as a signal that she wants to go out.

2. When your English Cocker Spaniel pup squats or hunches up on the floor, say nothing, but take a bit of the mess and put it on the paper. You don't need much, just enough to provide the scent of the urine or feces for the newspapers or training pads.

3. Take the puppy over to the paper and let it smell what's on it. You can usually remove the bait as soon as the puppy has smelled it; enough of the scent will remain to act as an attractant.

4. Repeating this several times will usually be enough to get your puppy to make the connection between going to the bathroom and using the paper, or training pad.

5. Be sure to pile on the praise as soon as your puppy uses the paper by itself. Don't let the papers get too dirty, though, pick up feces immediately and change the paper once the pup has used it for urination several times. If it gets too stinky, the puppy will avoid the spot.

6. You can start moving the paper closer to the outside as soon as the puppy uses it reliably, and most pups will soon catch on that they can use the yard as easily as they can their paper. Be sure to allow additional time for your English Cocker Spaniel to be reliably housetrained.

7. As with paper training, use some urine-soaked paper and a bit of feces in your yard where you want the pup to go, and this will be the place they will usually use. Be sure to pick up feces from the yard quickly; dogs don't like to go to the bathroom in a dirty place, and stepping in dog feces is singularly unpleasant.

In our experience with English Cocker Spaniel puppies, it only took a few times before they used the papers without fail. We were in the middle of a severe northern winter when we got them and didn't want to expose them to the cold while they were so young, and had little hair, so we actually let them use the papers longer than we ordinarily would have. As soon as the weather became warmer, they started using the yard without any problem, and none of them had any accidents in the house thereafter.

The 'Grab and Run' Technique

This technique can work quite well as long as you are in the home constantly. It will also depend not only on sticking to a tight schedule, but also on nearly continual observation of the puppy. As with the paper training method, it's important to establish a schedule the puppy can rely upon. Feeding the English Cocker Spaniel at the same times every day will start to regularize the puppy's digestive system. For a very young dog, always keep in mind that their digestion works on the principle of 'in one end, and out the other'.

1. As soon as the puppy has had a meal, or has even had a long drink, take it outside. In many cases, there will be results within a few minutes. Don't drag this out, however, if you've been outside for 10 minutes and nothing has happened, say nothing and bring the puppy back inside the home.

2. To begin with, puppies will simply urinate and defecate where they are. There is usually no warning when the bladder needs relief, and you should just resign yourself to cleaning up urine for a time. However, when a bowel movement is imminent, you may see your pup circling around and acting a bit agitated. Before the puppy actually starts to defecate, pick it up and take it outside. Lifting the puppy will cause a temporary interruption in the process, generally enough to allow you to get to the yard. Pet and praise the English Cocker Spaniel pup as soon as a deposit has been made in the yard.

3. If you see the puppy urinating, you can also pick it up and take it outside as quickly as possible. You may have to clean up a trail, but if the puppy does manage to finish urinating outside, be lavish with praise.

'Grab and Run' can be quite effective as a housetraining method as long as you are actually able to manage it. This will work best with those who work at home or those who are retired. Women who are homemakers can also take advantage of this technique to housetrain a new puppy. As with paper training, punishment or scolding has absolutely no place here, and will only be counterproductive.

Housetraining by Crate

Crate use for dogs and puppies has become something of a fad over the past few years, and some dog owners seem to view the crate as an essential piece of equipment. Crates can be useful for housetraining an English Cocker Spaniel, especially if the owner is unable to watch the puppy constantly. However, if you must be out of the house for an extended period, do not use the crate for housetraining. For those who do decide to use a crate to help housetrain their puppy, there are some factors that should always be kept in mind:

1. The size of the crate must fit the size of the puppy. A crate that is too small will be uncomfortable to the puppy, and could actually cause it to eliminate from stress. This will create a mess that you will have to clean up. A crate that is too large will also be a problem because there will be enough room for the puppy to use part of the crate as a bathroom without getting dirty itself.

2. When using a crate for housetraining, it's advisable to also feed the English Cocker Spaniel puppy in the crate. This should be done according to schedule, as you would if you were using any other housetraining method. Once the puppy has eaten, take it out of the crate and to the area where you wish it to eliminate. You will usually see results in a short period of time.

3. After the puppy has been brought back inside, put it into the crate again for about 20 minutes then take the pup outside again – your puppy will probably need another bathroom break then. Of course, if the weather is fine and you are able, you can stay outside with the puppy after it has first eliminated for some play, and to await the next call of nature.

The theory behind using a crate to housetrain an English Cocker Spaniel is that a crate of the proper size will discourage a puppy from soiling it, and the pup will learn to control itself, at least a little bit, in time for you to take it outside. This method, like the previous, requires you to be on hand during the day to constantly monitor the pup and see that a schedule is adhered to. You should never expect that you can pack the puppy into a crate, leave for the day and come back to let the pup out after you've finished with your peregrinations – you will only come back to a crate filled with feces and urine, and probably a very dirty, smelly, and unhappy English Cocker Spaniel puppy.

Handling Accidents

You should always be realistic about the probability of accidents. We have been lucky, but most owners will have to deal with house soiling even after it was considered that housetraining had been completed. Once again, do not react in any way other than to clean up after the animal; forget the rolled up newspaper or other forms of punishment, the puppy will have no idea why you are hurting them. It's also quite possible that you left the puppy alone for too long a time or it just became anxious – separation anxiety is a big cause of accidents.

The urine or feces should be removed immediately, and the area completely cleaned. You may want to use ordinary soap or detergent and hot water to clean up, and this is a good way to begin, but the organic compounds in the waste will continue to provide odor signals to the puppy unless you use an enzyme cleaner. Enzymes will break down and eliminate the telltale smells and make it much less likely that the pup will be attracted to the spot in the future. You may have to repeat the enzyme treatment several times. Never use ammonia to clean up the spot; it will only exacerbate the problem.

Male English Cocker Spaniels will sometimes begin to engage in marking behavior when they are about 5 months old. This is an instinctive reaction to staking out a territory. If you have decided to neuter the puppy, this should take care of the problem, but if you are leaving your male English Cocker Spaniel intact and the problem persists, consider using a belly-band to control him. The belly-band will prevent him from performing the 'ceremony' that accompanies marking behavior, and positive reinforcement for urinating outside will probably eliminate the problem entirely in short order.

Look upon an accident as a 'one-off' occurrence, and simply keep up with whatever housetraining procedure you have been using. In all likelihood, the puppy will revert to using the outdoors or papers again without any problem.

Accidents are quite likely when you first bring your new English Cocker Spaniel adult or puppy into the home. Expect that the pup will urinate. This is caused by excitement and/or the desire to claim the new location, and usually will not be repeated. Say nothing and clean up the mess, preferably with an enzyme based solution.

Housetraining accidents can also occur when a puppy or dog has been very ill. We have seen this in our English Cocker Spaniels when they required hospitalization for a severe illness. For some time afterwards, they were unable to control their bladders, especially when they were receiving subcutaneous fluids. Once they recovered, the problem vanished. I have never viewed these episodes as housetraining accidents, since the dog has been completely unable to control its bladder. This can definitely make it difficult if your dog is used to sleeping with you; we got around the problem by putting a piece of plastic under the area where our English Cocker Spaniel was going to sleep and covering it with a large rag that could either be washed or tossed.

Housetraining an Adult English Cocker Spaniel

Housetraining for an adult English Cocker Spaniel that you bring into the home is basically the same as you would use for a puppy, although you will probably not use paper training. Keep in mind that some adult dogs, especially those from shelters, could well have some mental or physical conditions that might make training more difficult. You may be pleased to find out that your new family member is already housetrained and nothing more is necessary than to introduce it to the yard. However, there can also be times when you will need to actively housetrain your adult dog, and the steps to do so are not difficult to follow:

1. Begin by establishing an eating and elimination schedule right away; taking the dog outside every 2 hours is appropriate. This will help to regularize the dog's system and make it less likely that there will be accidents. It will also help if you give your adult dog 2 smaller meals a day, rather than only 1 large one. This keeps the digestive system more likely to be reliable.

2. As with a puppy, there may be an initial urination to mark territory, but this usually will not occur again and should be cleaned up without comment or fuss on your part. The adult English Cocker Spaniel is in a completely unfamiliar situation that it doesn't understand and will take some time to adjust.

3. The more you are able to be around your adult English Cocker Spaniel, the more likely that it will quickly comply with your housetraining wishes. Once again, rely on positive reinforcement for a job well done, rather than punishment.

4. If you change your English Cocker Spaniel's diet abruptly, it could cause it to develop diarrhea. This could cause unintentional accidents. When changing your English Cocker Spaniel's food, do so gradually to allow its body to adjust.

4th Chapter: Crate Training

Since dog crates are now looked upon as being an absolute necessity if you have a puppy or dog, it's amazing that dog owners were able to do without them for thousands of years and still have happy, well-trained dogs. Be that as it may, crate training is now looked upon as being essential to keeping a dog; as important as food, water, attention, and veterinary care.

It is quite true that many dogs prefer to find a small, secure spot in which to sleep or relax, and a crate can provide this – as long as the door is kept open. Once the door of the crate is closed, it becomes a species of cage or prison. Crate training can help in housetraining, confining the dog while in transit or during an emergency, or when trying to correct destructive behavior. However, those who view the crate as a place in which to leave a puppy or dog for hours on end should consider whether they are really prepared to own a dog.

English Cocker Spaniels are social animals, and require companionship and interaction with humans. One may ask, what is the point of acquiring an English Cocker Spaniel, or any breed of dog, if the animal is going to spend long hours confined in a crate? One of the major reasons for getting a dog is to have a companion.

If you purchase an English Cocker Spaniel adult or puppy from a breeder outside your immediate area, it will likely be shipped to you in a crate. You can use this crate to begin training, as it is probably an appropriate size for the animal. Acquisition of a pet from a local breeder or from rescue or a shelter will probably require that you purchase a crate yourself. There are several varieties of crate: wire, cloth sided, and plastic. The plastic crates generally consist of upper and lower sections that are held together with screws, and this type of crate may prove the easiest to use when you are beginning crate training.

There is no way to 'cheap out' when buying a crate for a puppy. You should purchase one that fits the pup's size and continue buying new crates that fit the puppy until it is an adult. Your English Cocker Spaniel should be able to turn around in the crate and have enough space to stand and to lie down comfortably. There are problems with crates that are either too big or too small:

1. A crate that is too small denies your English Cocker Spaniel the ability to stand up, turn around, or even settle down normally. The only thing the dog will want to do is to get out of it as quickly as possible. This situation often arises when owners don't want to spend money on progressively larger crates as their puppy grows. If purchasing successive crates is beyond your financial resources, then simply don't bother with a crate at all.

2. Crates much larger than needed present their own problems. Many owners think that they can 'get away' with buying a crate that will fit the adult dog, leaving the puppy in a room, in effect. With so much space, the puppy will usually choose to use part of the crate as a bathroom, especially if it's left in the crate for an extended period of time – it can just retreat to the farther end away from the mess.

One important thing to remember is that you should never use the crate as punishment. Your English Cocker Spaniel adult or puppy will do all in its power to avoid using it, and will probably be noisy until you let it out. Animals that are crated as punishment will often eliminate due to stress, which will only mean that you will have a very unpleasant cleaning up to handle, possibly including the dog.

Beginning English Cocker Spaniel Crate Training

Unless your English Cocker Spaniel arrived in a crate, and often even if it did, you will have to get the animal accustomed to it. You can probably count on the natural curiosity of dogs to begin investigating the crate right away. If you have a plastic crate, it's a good idea to remove the top half to make the crate seem less threatening and enclosing. Once your English Cocker Spaniel seems comfortable with the open-topped crate, you can put the top half back on again, but still keep the door open. Let the puppy or dog explore the crate for several days, and become used to it before you start any actual crate training. Puppies are a good deal more likely to 'take' to their crate before than will an adult dog that has never before been confined.

It's important where you place the crate in your home. If you place it several rooms away from where the family gathers, it will not only be inconvenient, but the dog will feel isolated and lonely. The crate should be where the dog can see people, at the minimum. You can put it under a table or between several pieces of furniture so that it won't be so obtrusive.

You must make the crate appear both unthreatening and appealing to your English Cocker Spaniel:

1. If you can remove the top half of the crate, do so, and start putting treats in the crate to entice the dog to enter on its own.

2. Either remove the door temporarily or tie it open so that it doesn't accidentally close and startle your English Cocker Spaniel.

3. Provide comfortable bedding in the crate so that your English Cocker Spaniel will enjoy lying down inside it. Remember to change the bedding every week – dogs actually like something clean to lie down on.

4. Praise your English Cocker Spaniel whenever it goes into the crate on its own.

5. Feed your English Cocker Spaniel adult or puppy in the crate.

6. If the animal is too frightened of the crate to actually eat inside it, place the food dish outside near the crate. As the dog becomes used to the crate, you can move the food dish inside. The water dish should also be placed inside; one that attaches to the door of the crate will help prevent spillage.

Take all these steps slowly and never display any impatience or anger if things are not going as you believe they should.

Once the dog seems to be comfortable in the crate, and going into it freely, you can begin closing the door. At this point, don't latch it, so that if your English Cocker Spaniel panics, it can just push out again. Only leave the door closed for a minute or two and gradually work up to longer periods, eventually latching the door. Always remember to put treats and toys into the crate and also to praise and treat after a successful period in the crate.

Crating for Housebreaking

Crates can be useful for housetraining your English Cocker Spaniel. You can begin using the crate for this once your pet has become used to the crate and is eating in it regularly. Place both food and water dishes in the crate. Water should be available to your English Cocker Spaniel at all times, but you should feed your pup on a schedule as soon as you welcome it into the house. Very young puppies will do best with 4 meals per day, and it's advisable to feed adult English Cocker Spaniels smaller meals twice a day rather than one enormous meal. This helps to keep the energy levels of your English Cocker Spaniel high and will prevent it from becoming too hungry between feedings.

1. Put the food dish in the crate and close the door. A puppy will usually have to have a bowel movement soon after eating.

2. As soon as your puppy has finished eating, take it outside to eliminate.

3. It can take up to 10 minutes for results, so be patient.

4. If your English Cocker Spaniel puppy does nothing within this time period, take it back inside, put it back into the crate, and take it outside again in about 20 minutes.

5. Praise the puppy for a job well done when results are produced.

6. The same process should be applied to the pup's water dish – as soon as the puppy has had a drink, take it outside.

The theory behind using a crate for housebreaking is that canines instinctively avoid soiling where they sleep. However, if you leave your English Cocker Spaniel puppy in the crate for too long periods, especially after eating or drinking, there will be accidents. The same measures for housetraining will apply to an adult as they will to a puppy. Puppies that have grown up in a kennel situation are used to eliminating where they eat and sleep and will often use the crate to urinate and defecate, especially to begin with. Never punish your puppy for this, and try a different housetraining method for these pups, or keep an extremely close eye on what your English Cocker Spaniel puppy is doing.

Curbing Destructive Behavior

English Cocker Spaniel puppies and dogs can engage in activities that can cause damage and even destruction to the home and its furnishings. Puppies are probably the worst perpetrators of this because they are teething. To relieve the feelings of their irritated gums and assist the new teeth in breaking through, puppies will literally chew anything they can get their teeth on. In most cases, as we found ourselves, this destructive behavior will cease once the permanent teeth emerge. You can help to stop this inappropriate chewing if you provide acceptable chewing material for the puppy. We found that choo-hooves worked best for our pups – they enjoyed not only the hard texture that helped with their teething, but also the taste of the hoof.

Choo-hooves also stood up well to the strong jaws of our English Cocker Spaniel puppies. Keep in mind, however, that even if you provide a mountain of chewing toys, your English Cocker Spaniel may still gnaw on your furniture or footwear. It is always best to remove things you do not want chewed from the reach of your puppy. Bad tasting sprays or liquids are available to put onto furniture, but one of our dogs actually developed a taste for bitter apple.

Some English Cocker Spaniels will also continue inappropriate chewing behavior into adulthood. Destructive chewing in this case often arises from separation anxiety when the owner leaves the home. This occurs because of the strong feelings that the dog has for its owner; wild canids tend to 'pal around' with one another constantly, so being alone is a hardship for most dogs. The English Cocker Spaniel will often relieve its anxiety by chewing up furniture, rugs, curtains, or anything else within reach. You will be surprised at how much trouble these canines can deliver.

Crating for destructive behavior, to keep your English Cocker Spaniel confined when you, the owner, are not in the home, should only be used as a last resort. Never use the crate as punishment when damage has been discovered – you have to find a solution to the problem rather than discipline the dog.

Other ways of handling separation anxiety will be addressed later in this book. If the owner absolutely must use the crate to keep the dog from tearing up the house, the English Cocker Spaniel must first be completely familiarized with the crate to begin with – no owner should think that they can simply stuff their pet into the crate before leaving for the day with happy results; you could easily find a damaged crate and an injured dog upon your return.

If your English Cocker Spaniel has accepted the crate and you are going to use this to confine the dog while you are at work, it might be a good idea to hire a pet sitter to come during the day to let the dog out to use the yard and stretch its legs. Any dog that is going to be left alone for more than 4 hours should be visited by a pet sitter or neighbor midway through the day; could you avoid using the toilet for 8 or 10 hours? Confining a dog for too long a period is not only cruel; it can easily result in a crate full of urine and stools.

English Cocker Spaniels are not the best candidates for long term crate confinement, and leaving your dog in a crate, day after day, could easily lead to behavior problems. Another alternative can be to have a friend or relative take care of your English Cocker Spaniel while you're at work; this will guarantee that your dog gets the human companionship it needs and leads a more normal life.

Like most dogs, English Cocker Spaniels will often become destructive when they are deprived of mental and/or physical stimulation. English Cocker Spaniels need exercise and stimulation every day, and providing these can help to prevent destructive behavior from arising in the first place.

Taking your English Cocker Spaniel on a walk, as long as the weather is not excessively hot, can help to satisfy its exercise needs. It doesn't have to be a long walk either, around the block or down the street and back home will be fine. Playing with your English Cocker Spaniel can also keep it mentally and physically sound, as can teaching your English Cocker Spaniel tricks, something that will be addressed later in this book.

Owners sometimes, in the hope of prolonging the life of their pet, will put their English Cocker Spaniel on a very restrictive diet. Some English Cocker Spaniels will actually become destructive because they are looking for something to eat. They will break into dog food bags or attack the garbage if they have not gotten enough to eat. If the English Cocker Spaniel's ribs are showing or you can feel them too easily, it's likely that it is acting up simply because it is hungry. Try increasing the amount of food you are feeding your English Cocker Spaniel, and the desperate chewing may stop. Space the meals out over the day so that it will be less likely to get peckish. Yes, English Cocker Spaniels do have a propensity to overeat and can become obese, but half starving them is not the answer, either. If you are undecided on what and how much to feed your English Cocker Spaniel every day, speak with your veterinarian.

When a Crate Should Never Be Used

Many people find crates useful with regards to their English Cocker Spaniel, but there are situations when your English Cocker Spaniel should never be placed into the crate:

1. Sick animals should never be confined. The only exception to this is if your English Cocker Spaniel is being treated for heartworm, and its activity must be severely curtailed to prevent further damage to your English Cocker Spaniel's heart or lungs. Putting a sick animal in a crate is simply cruel and could seriously interfere with an animal that is in pain from finding a comfortable position.

2. An English Cocker Spaniel with diarrhea is a disaster in the making if placed in a crate; likewise an English Cocker Spaniel with a urinary infection. English Cocker Spaniels suffering from these conditions will be unable to control their elimination and will only soil the crate and themselves. The body has absolutely no ability to hold in liquid feces.

3. Hot weather is another time when your English Cocker Spaniel should not be crated. Confinement in a crate during extreme heat can lead to dehydration and heat stroke. Your English Cocker Spaniel could die quickly under these conditions.

4. An English Cocker Spaniel that has damaged the crate in its attempts to escape should not be confined; eventually the dog will also injure itself. If you find part of the crate has been chewed, it is signaling a desperate English Cocker Spaniel. When one of our girls was shipped to us, we found that her little paws were all scored and cut where she had tried to dig out of the shipping crate, which was relegated to the barn immediately. These were relatively minor injuries – dogs can break teeth or even their jaws or tear out their claws attempting to escape from a crate.

5. English Cocker Spaniels with separation anxiety will not do well if confined to a crate; it will only magnify these feelings and make the problem worse. Putting an English Cocker Spaniel with separation anxiety into a little box is basically inhuman.

6. If you live in an apartment house or in a neighborhood where the homes are close together, your neighbors will certainly let you know if your dog has been barking or howling for hours on end. In this case, do not crate your English Cocker Spaniel again. English Cocker Spaniels will bark nonstop for hours if they dislike being in a crate.

When to Give Up

Some English Cocker Spaniels will accustom themselves to a crate without any fuss, and although I am not one who believes in the use of a crate except when the door is kept open at all times (or for emergencies or when traveling), this will be an issue between the owner and the dog. Remember, you do not have to use a crate – it could well be that manufacturers and retailers of crates have pushed this 'crate agenda' on dog owners, but there is absolutely nothing that dictates that you must use a crate at all. In my opinion it is nothing more than a fad, and hopefully will disappear as soon as possible.

However, some English Cocker Spaniel puppies and dogs will never become used to being confined in a crate – these dogs will constantly whine, bark, howl, drool, claw, or chew at the crate to get out. And, the solution is to let them out. There is no law or universal rule that states that crate training is somehow necessary to the health or wellbeing of a dog.

A client of mine had a toy dog that was well behaved and completely housetrained, yet she thought that she 'had' to keep her dog in the crate during the day because it seemed to be the accepted practice. The dog whined constantly for months on end, and was completely unable to accept being kept in the crate, even though it was placed next to her chair. One has to ask oneself, why bother? What was the point in keeping a well-behaved dog in the crate at all?

What is the point of having a dog if you are going to confine it to a crate, especially if you put your English Cocker Spaniel in a crate while you are in the home? As far as sleeping arrangements go, many 'authorities' state that dogs should be confined in their crate at night. This is wrong – your English Cocker Spaniel should either sleep in your bed with you or sleep in a bed next to yours.

English Cocker Spaniels are not automatons or robots, they are intelligent, emotional living creatures that have evolved with humans and should be treated with the respect they deserve. We have found, with our English Cocker Spaniels that sleeping in bed with us has completely negated the theory that dogs will bite when awakened suddenly. They may do so because they are sleeping alone and so are insecure and will react fearfully when touched 'out of the blue', but if you think about it, dogs and wild canines nearly always sleep together. If the normal reaction to be jostled when asleep was to attack, there would be little sleeping done as there would be constant fights. Dogs get used to being touched when asleep under more natural conditions and don't react at all, shuffle a bit to one side to make room, or perhaps open a bleary eye. My dogs have even shared my pillow without any problem.

5th Chapter: Obedience Training

After housebreaking, obedience is the training considered to be the most important by dog owners. One thing that every owner should keep in mind is that a great deal of their English Cocker Spaniel's 'bad behavior' actually stems from them, not from the English Cocker Spaniel itself. Obedience training is actually not only about training the dog; it's about training you, the owner, to also act in a certain way. We humans tend to look upon anything the dog does wrong as being the dog's fault. To a certain extent, it undoubtedly is, but in many cases, the human partner has acted in the role of enabler, whether consciously or not. Raising an English Cocker Spaniel in a responsible manner is just as important as raising a child well.

Patience, time, consistency, goals, and more patience are required for successfully obedience training an English Cocker Spaniel. Always remember that the level of trainability will vary from individual dog to individual dog. All breeds have their characteristics that form the foundation of the mental and physical makeup of the dog, but breeding practices and environmental conditions, as well as what might just be termed the 'innate quirkiness' of some dogs can skew expectations. The receptiveness of the English Cocker Spaniel to training is actually unrelated to the actual intelligence of a dog – some dogs have evolved to do multiple tasks or as hunting dogs and will be very receptive to training. Dogs which have historically been used for only one job can be more difficult to train. From my own experience, English Cocker Spaniels can present some obedience training challenges, in part because they do have a good measure of the stubbornness that is found in dogs of all sizes.

Obedience training can obviously be carried out by the owner, and this is what happens in most cases, and this can help to make the bond between you and your English Cocker Spaniel all the stronger. However, there are professional trainers and behaviorists that can also be used to provide the training needed, especially when difficulties arise. Owners who avail themselves of professionals for training should realize that they will have to continue with some level of follow-up to maintain the training over time so that their English Cocker Spaniel does not 'forget' what it has learned. If you never use the 'Come' command for over a year, it's not too likely that your English Cocker Spaniel will respond when you finally do. You can make refresher lessons into a game too.

Why Obedience Train?

Owners may well ask, "Why bother to obedience train my English Cocker Spaniel at all?" And this is a valid question, after all this does take time, dedication, and a high level of involvement. Even the amenable English Cocker Spaniel can exhibit unwanted behavior that can make it less than an attractive and valued companion.

Obedience training is simply a good idea for several reasons:

1. An English Cocker Spaniel that is well-trained will be able to go more places with its owner – it will understand how to behave when confronted by strange situations and people. A trained dog will be much less likely to be startled and remain calm wherever it is, and you will not have to worry so much about it behaving in an inappropriate or aggressive manner; and yes, English Cocker Spaniels have teeth and know how to use them if they feel it is necessary.

2. Obedience training can keep your English Cocker Spaniel safer. All of us who own dogs know that there are times when the dog will act unpredictably – such as running out in the road unexpectedly. Even if you keep your English Cocker Spaniel on a leash when out of the home, dogs can sometimes just dart out

when a door is opened, or escape from a fenced yard. If your English Cocker Spaniel has learned to 'stay' when directed, it's likely that it will at least hesitate before proceeding into traffic and give you the opportunity to reach it.

3. Well-trained English Cocker Spaniels tend to be more confident. They understand their relationship with their owner better, and are not as prone to fear or fear aggression in comparison to dogs that have been allowed to 'run wild'. Some English Cocker Spaniels are aware of their comparative size in relation to other dogs and people. This can affect their emotions and behavior around others. Obedience training can help to overcome this tendency. Conversely, some English Cocker Spaniels will consider that they are the biggest dog going and will challenge larger or potentially dangerous dogs.

Starting Early

As with the young of any species, an English Cocker Spaniel puppy will be much more malleable and trainable than will an adult English Cocker Spaniel. From about the age of 8 to 12 weeks, your new puppy will be at the best age to form a strong bond with you, and will be especially receptive to your training program. As the old saying goes, "Strike while the iron is hot." Use this development window not only to bond with your English Cocker Spaniel, but to begin training.

However, when starting obedience training at an early age with your puppy, you should be aware that the puppy is still a puppy, and will not only be full of energy and mischief, but also will have a relatively short attention span. You will require a few pieces of equipment for training: collar or harness, long leash, and treats. There are a few commands that you can start teaching your puppy as soon as it comes into your home:

1. Sit

2. Stay

3. Come

4. Down

These 4 commands will actually be sufficient for most English Cocker Spaniels to go through their life with; they will allow you to control your English Cocker Spaniel in most situations. These commands are also the foundation of more advanced commands that might be needed or desired.

Because the puppy's attention span will be relatively short, keep the sessions short too – 10 or 15 minutes is long enough. You can conduct several obedience training sessions during the day rather than one long one, and always remember to be lavish with praise and treats when the pup does well. Completely ignore mistakes; calling your English Cocker Spaniel puppy out for an error will only provide negative attention and make it more likely for that error to be repeated. Use obedience training as a way to establish trust in you and confidence in your puppy.

It's not only the puppy's attention span that should receive attention; your attention span and the limits of your patience are also important. Training an English Cocker Spaniel puppy to do even simple commands like 'sit' can take dozens of repetitions, and if you get frustrated, your puppy will pick up on this and be even more difficult to train. As soon as you start feeling frustrated or angry, even if your puppy still seems ready to continue, stop the training immediately. Treat your puppy and spend some time playing with it so that it will look upon obedience training favorably. Like with any other dog breed, English Cocker Spaniels can sometimes not be the easiest dogs to train, but they can be trained successfully if you are willing to put the effort into it.

Not everyone will be starting with a puppy, however, many dogs are adopted when they are older, either from a breeder looking to get rid of extra animals, or from rescue groups and shelters.

Because your adult English Cocker Spaniel will inevitably be coming with some mental and/or physical 'baggage', you may have to spend more time training an adult than you would a puppy. When adopting an adult English Cocker Spaniel, give it a bit of time to settle into the new surroundings before you begin active training. Once again, relying exclusively on positive reinforcement for obedience training will produce the best and most reliable results.

Basic Obedience Training for Your English Cocker Spaniel

It's best, to begin with, to choose a spot to train your English Cocker Spaniel where there will be few distractions; this will allow both of you to concentrate on the training. You don't necessarily have to use the exact same place every day, and it's probably a good idea to switch the locations, too, so that your English Cocker Spaniel adult or puppy doesn't come to associate obedience with just one place, but as something that is to be followed everywhere.

"Sit"

The "Sit" command is probably a good place to start; it's something your pet does naturally and requires little effort on your part or your English Cocker Spaniel's. Kneel or use a chair or stool to keep you at approximately the level of your English Cocker Spaniel. Use a leash to keep your English Cocker Spaniel from backing up during this lesson.

1. Hold a treat just above your English Cocker Spaniel's nose so that it gets a good sniff, and then move it over its head towards the back of its body. Make sure you keep the leash short.

2. This motion will cause your English Cocker Spaniel to lower its rump as long as it cannot back up since the leash is preventing backward movement.

3. Once your English Cocker Spaniel's rump touches the floor, say "Sit" and give your English Cocker Spaniel the treat immediately. The point here is to get your pup to associate the word with sitting and receiving a treat.

4. You can do this several times, but don't repeat until your English Cocker Spaniel adult or puppy becomes bored and frustrated. When its eyes start to wander or it seems fidgety, break off the lesson.

5. Spread lessons over the course of the day to keep them interesting. If you're like most people, you probably found your school days boring to one extent or another, and this interfered with your learning ability; the same will be true with your English Cocker Spaniel, if it becomes bored, it simply will not absorb the lesson.

6. This will generally achieve good results within a short period of time, and your English Cocker Spaniel will learn to "Sit" without any other control than your voice – you will not have to dangle treats over its head.

"Stay"

You don't need to wait until the pup or dog has mastered "Sit" before adding "Stay" to the lessons. This command may take more work than "Sit" due to your English Cocker Spaniel puppy's desire to be with you, so have patience.

1. When your English Cocker Spaniel is in the "Sit" position, start moving away from it slowly, while repeating the word "Stay". You can make motions with your hand to encourage your English Cocker Spaniel to remain in that position.

2. If your English Cocker Spaniel remains in position when you have gone even a slight distance from it, treat and praise. Try to reward your English Cocker Spaniel before it actually starts to get up.

3. Gradually lengthen the distance from your sitting English Cocker Spaniel, all the while giving the proper command.

4. When your English Cocker Spaniel breaks the "Stay" command, simply return it to "Sit" and try again.

5. Break off the lesson at the first sign of frustration on the part of either participant. This lesson can be repeated several times during the day – short, more frequent lessons are much more effective than long, drawn-out ones.

"Come"

"Come" may be one of the easier commands for your English Cocker Spaniel pup or adult to master; it wants to be with you, after all, so just build on this natural attraction for successful lessons. You will need a flat collar and long leash for this lesson.

1. Attach the collar and leash and put your English Cocker Spaniel in the "Sit" position.

2. Give the "Stay" command.

3. Move several feet away from your pup and say "Come". Chances are that your English Cocker Spaniel will move towards you, and be sure to treat and praise. Squatting down, rather than standing, will make your English Cocker Spaniel even more eager to come to you.

4. If your English Cocker Spaniel seems reluctant to approach you, give a small tug on the leash to get it moving, this is not any kind of correction, rather to just get your dog's attention. Do not drag your English Cocker Spaniel towards you, this sends a negative message, such as anger. If your English Cocker Spaniel comes upon receiving the cue, treat and praise.

The important things to remember when giving basic obedience training is to keep the training sessions short, especially for puppies, and always use positive reinforcement, in the form of treats and praise, to reward success. It will take numerous repetitions, in most cases, for your companion to understand what you want and to learn to respond to your commands. Never allow yourself to become angry with your English Cocker Spaniel, it is counterproductive.

It's quite possible that you will run into some bumps and stops while training your English Cocker Spaniel. English Cocker Spaniels can easily become tyrants in the home. Due to their bond with their English Cocker Spaniel, owners can often allow them to get away with more bad behavior without realizing. Of course, it is extremely unlikely that anyone in the family home will be seriously harmed by your English Cocker Spaniel, although they could injure a small child, but do you really want to live with a dog that growls and snaps, or even bites when it doesn't get its own way? Obedience training is one way to prevent this from happening without having to come down heavily on your English Cocker Spaniel. Preventing problems in the first place is always much easier than trying to correct them.

Once a training session has been completed, spend some time playing with your pup so that it will come to look upon these sessions as a prelude to a good time. Remember that the best time for training to be conducted is while your English Cocker Spaniel is young; not only because it will be most impressionable then, but also because negative behavior patterns have not been fixed.

Advanced Techniques

Once your English Cocker Spaniel has been reliably trained for basic obedience, you might want to train it for more difficult training objectives. These are also valuable tools for helping your English Cocker Spaniel behave well in a variety of situations, and once the basic techniques have been mastered, you will probably find it easier for both of you to proceed to the next training steps – both of you will have become trained.

"Down"

Placing an English Cocker Spaniel in the "Down" position can be looked upon as the first of the more advanced obedience techniques. This will help your English Cocker Spaniel behave better both in the home and outside of it. It can help to calm an overexcited English Cocker Spaniel, or keep one that is injured or ill quieter. However, keep in mind that your English Cocker Spaniel will look upon this as being a submissive position for it to be in, and may resist it more than it would the basic obedience commands.

Previously, it had been taught that the way to teach down was to force your English Cocker Spaniel down by using the pressure of your foot on its leash, but this method should be avoided – it will only intensify your English Cocker Spaniel's feeling of helplessness, or could spark aggression. This technique can be used when your English Cocker Spaniel is either sitting (the easiest since the dog is halfway there) or standing.

1. Get your English Cocker Spaniel into the "Sit" position. Place a treat in front of its nose and lower the treat to the floor. The English Cocker Spaniel will naturally lower itself. As your English Cocker Spaniel's body touches the floor, say "Down".

2. You will, of course, have to repeat this exercise quite a few times, but as long as you keep treating your English Cocker Spaniel and giving it praise, "Down" will become part of your English Cocker Spaniel's repertoire.

3. After your English Cocker Spaniel has taken the treat while lying down, use another treat to bring it back to the sitting position, and repeat the lesson.

4. It can be a bit harder to get your English Cocker Spaniel to lie down if it's standing, but repeated practice, using treats and praise will train your English Cocker Spaniel to obey your command.

5. As always, suspend practice when your English Cocker Spaniel's attention begins to wander.

"Heel"

There has been quite a bit of discussion over the past few years about whether it really is necessary to teach your English Cocker Spaniel to "Heel". Some trainers advocate letting your dog circulate around you, within a narrow radius, rather than stick to your left side. While there may be some validity to this new train of thought, it does relinquish control of the dog to a considerable degree, which could prove to be problematic in certain situations. By teaching your English Cocker Spaniel to heel, you will be keeping the human member of the partnership in the leadership position and make the dog easier to control. Teaching an English Cocker Spaniel (or any dog breed) to heel is difficult, but it can be done with time, patience, consistency, and treats. Unless you plan never to take your English Cocker Spaniel anywhere at all, especially around other people and dogs, teaching it to heel is essential.

You won't need much equipment to teach your English Cocker Spaniel to heel; harness or flat collar (depending on whether a collar can slip over the dog's head), leash, treats, and perhaps a piece of tape. You can actually teach your English Cocker Spaniel to heel without using a leash, but most people find it more convenient to use one.

Choke collars, shock collars, or prong collars are not necessary to teach any dog to behave properly on leash, they only cause unnecessary distress to the dog and are an unneeded form of negative reinforcement. Always remember that the leash is not to be used to yank on the dog, it's only there to keep it from straying during the lesson.

1. Stand with your English Cocker Spaniel on your left side. Hold the end of the leash in your right hand. The slack will be taken up by your left hand. This provides you, in effect, with a very short leash, and this makes it much easier for you to control your English Cocker Spaniel. You should also keep some treats in your left hand, out of sight, and they mustn't have a smell that your English Cocker Spaniel is able to easily detect.

2. Say your English Cocker Spaniel's name to get its attention. Your English Cocker Spaniel should make eye contact with you. If it doesn't look up at you, you can touch the top of its head to draw its notice.

3. Tell your English Cocker Spaniel to "Sit", then say "Heel" and take two steps forward. If nothing else, your English Cocker Spaniel will probably follow the scent of the treats. If your English Cocker Spaniel follows you, treat and praise it.

4. If your English Cocker Spaniel doesn't follow you, step back and repeat the heel command, perhaps holding the treat closer to your English Cocker Spaniel's nose. Remember that this is something completely new to your dog and it will take a while for this lesson to be learned.

5. Repeat the two steps forward until your English Cocker Spaniel can do this reliably, then increase the distance by two steps. Every time your English Cocker Spaniel is able to follow the "Heel" command, increase the distance.

6. Vary the lessons after your pet is able to heel on command over a distance of 20 feet or so, by making turns or going around corners. Remember to practice these new additions one at a time until your English Cocker Spaniel is comfortable doing them. As training progresses and your English Cocker Spaniel heels well, try introducing distractions such as the neighbor's children or

another dog. If your English Cocker Spaniel shows any inclination to break the command, repeat "Heel" and direct your English Cocker Spaniel to "Sit" to get it back to its mental starting point. Once it sits down, say "Heel", and continue as before.

7. As your English Cocker Spaniel becomes more proficient in heeling, you can start cutting back on the treats; eventually you will rely entirely on the command and a word of praise.

Ideally, training your English Cocker Spaniel to heel will proceed without any problem, but only the most rosy-eyed optimist would think that, and most of you will experience a glitch or two along the way. Unless you have a particularly stubborn English Cocker Spaniel, it will learn to heel in time. Intimidating your English Cocker Spaniel will not work (and could serve to make it aggressive), stick with positive reinforcement and things will work out, although you should be prepared to work with your English Cocker Spaniel for a long period of time when teaching this. There are some common problems that will often arise during training, however:

1. If your English Cocker Spaniel just doesn't seem to be paying attention to your left side, stick a bit of tape onto your side, at the height of your English Cocker Spaniel's head – this will often be enough to help it focus on where it should be.

2. Don't be surprised if your pup lunges forward as it usually does when on leash. Don't pull on the leash or yell, simply stand firm. Your English Cocker Spaniel is on a very short lead (or it should be) and won't be able to go far. Turn your body in the opposite direction; your English Cocker Spaniel will have to follow without the need of any obvious force on your part. Give your English Cocker Spaniel the "Heel" command again, and if it remains at your side, take two steps forward and treat if your English Cocker Spaniel follows.

3. You can also use the 'stand and turn' if your English Cocker Spaniel has become distracted by something and tries to wander away.

4. English Cocker Spaniels that have become bored make very poor pupils and if you see your English Cocker Spaniel yawning or becoming obstinate, suspend the lesson – continuing it when your English Cocker Spaniel refuses will just reinforces your pet's stubborn behavior. Needless to say, don't give your English Cocker Spaniel a treat now.

Once your English Cocker Spaniel has mastered the "Heel" command you will be able to confidently take it with you wherever you go. Not all English Cocker Spaniels will learn at the same level of speed, and some may need much more intensive work than others. The key is to be liberal with praise and treats, and to break off a session when either of you is becoming frustrated. A younger dog will, of course, be quicker to catch on to what you want, but a dog of any age will be able to learn this command if you are willing to take the time and effort to teach it.

Obedience Classes

Puppy or dog obedience classes are another training option that has worked well for many people who own English Cocker Spaniels. These are classes that can be a good idea in a number of ways: you and your English Cocker Spaniel will be doing the lessons together, and your pup or adult English Cocker Spaniel will learn how to get on better with other dogs and with strange people. Be sure that your pet's vaccinations are up to date before enrolling in a class, and never take your dog there if it is showing any signs of illness.

Although most people who opt for classes do just fine with a group arrangement, there are times when the owner may want to schedule private training classes. An English Cocker Spaniel that has serious behavioral problems should not be in a group class, nor should an English Cocker Spaniel that is showing a high level of fear and anxiety. In these cases, an animal behaviorist can help you work with your pet to overcome their problems and become obedience trained. A fearful or aggressive English Cocker Spaniel will be more likely to keep itself under control when it has become more confident through obedience training.

To Use a Trainer, Or Not To Use a Trainer?

Sometimes, an owner either doesn't have the time, knowledge, or patience to provide adequate obedience training for their English Cocker Spaniel. An unruly English Cocker Spaniel, even a small one that is displaying problem behavior, will often wind up in a shelter unless some kind of training is provided to help the animal learn how to adjust itself to the household. While training your English Cocker Spaniel yourself is obviously the best answer since it helps to establish a close relationship between you and your English Cocker Spaniel, a trainer can be used if necessary, and is certainly an option if you are ready to give up on your English Cocker Spaniel.

There are some very important things to understand when you are considering a trainer, and the first is that there are no laws or statutes that control dog training – literally anyone can call themselves a dog trainer regardless of how competent or skilled they actually are. You can run into a trainer that is absolutely the top in their field, or a total incompetent that will harm your dog. Before you consign your English Cocker Spaniel adult or puppy over to a trainer, there are some things that should be checked beforehand:

1. Ask to inspect the trainer's facility. It should be clean, at the very least; a place that stinks of dog feces and urine, or that has piles of garbage around is not a place you want to leave your English Cocker Spaniel.

2. Ask the trainer if he or she has any kind of certification or has attended any seminars on dog training, these could lend some credence as to their ability to train your English Cocker Spaniel.

3. Pin the trainer down on exactly what kind of training methods will be used – a red flag should go up if the person is vague about this; he or she probably doesn't know what they are doing and are just looking to make a quick buck.

4. Ask what kind of training equipment will be used, if any; mention of shock collars, prong collars, nose boppers, or choke collars should have you heading out the door as quickly as your feet can carry you.

5. Any trainer who mentions that your English Cocker Spaniel might have to be euthanized should be avoided. This person obviously has no affinity for dogs and could well harm your English Cocker Spaniel.

6. A trainer who claims that their results are guaranteed will literally be 'talking out of the other side of their hat'. Even the best trainer will not absolutely be able to produce completely positive results with every dog - there are simply too many factors involved for promises of this kind to be made.

7. Pay attention to your instincts about the trainer. If the person makes you uncomfortable, look elsewhere for help. Someone who seems 'creepy', loud-mouthed, or aggressive is not someone with whom you want to leave your English Cocker Spaniel. Any trainer who makes even the vaguest of sexual overtures to you should be avoided immediately.

8. If the potential trainer seems to be under the influence of alcohol or drugs, vacate the premises immediately.

Even if you find the perfect trainer who fulfills your every expectation, you will still have to use the commands your English Cocker Spaniel has been taught on a regular basis – the dog will simply become accustomed to not hearing and obeying the commands if you don't use them. You certainly shouldn't expect your English Cocker Spaniel to heel perfectly if it hasn't heard the command for 10 months; keeping your English Cocker Spaniel current on the lessons learned will be up to you, unless you want to keep returning your English Cocker Spaniel to the trainer for refresher courses.

Training Collars

There are a number of different kinds of collars or harnesses that are used for training dogs. You will be using either a harness or a collar when teaching your English Cocker Spaniel obedience.

1. Flat collar. This is the old reliable leather or nylon collar that lies flat around the dog's neck; it is adjusted to the neck and will neither tighten nor loosen when on the puppy or dog. Attached to a leash, this collar provides a great deal of control over the animal. You should be able to get two fingers under the collar if it is adjusted correctly. A collar that is too tight can restrict the dog's breathing and be uncomfortable, while one that is too large could just slip right over the head.

2. Choke collar. A choke collar is a length of metal chain with rings attached at either end. By slipping part of the collar through one of the rings, the owner will have a loop that can be fitted over the dog's head. A leash is attached to the free ring. These collars, unlike flat collars, can be easily tightened when the owner wishes to correct the dog. Pulling on the leash will cause the collar to squeeze the dog's throat. These collars should release immediately to allow the dog to breathe. The correction can be slight, mainly to draw the dog's attention, or sharp, to cause pain and restrict breathing temporarily. Choke collars can damage your English Cocker Spaniel's windpipe or spine, and they can also cause bruising.

3. Prong collars. Surely something out of torture chambers, prong collars are a species of modified choke collar with prongs on the inside. Like Martingale collars (used mostly for dogs with very narrow heads), prong collars are self-limited, and unlike choke collars, can only be tightened to a certain extent. There is obviously no way that this kind of collar will be used except to inflict pain on the animal during training. Pulling on the leash will tighten the prong collar, pressing the points into the dog's flesh. These collars can cause serious injury to an English Cocker Spaniel – in the past, the tracheas of dogs have been pierced by these collars.

4. Shock collars. Many trainers rely on shock collars when working with English Cocker Spaniels simply because the trainer does not have to be next to the dog for the collar to work, they have a variable range, depending on the collar. There are different 'correction' levels with most shock collars, ranging from a mild vibration to one step below electric chair. Some breeds will be able to ignore any 'stimulation', rendering the collar completely useless. Shock collars have a small box with prongs that are fitted so that the prongs are just pressing against the center of the English Cocker Spaniel's throat (contact with the dog's flesh is necessary if the shock is to be felt). These collars should only be left on for a short period of time. They can cause irritation and even burns to the skin if overused.

5. Front clip harnesses. Most harnesses have the attachment for the leash over the dog's shoulders. While the most common of harnesses, it also makes control of the animal more difficult. Front clip harnesses have the leash ring in the front, right under the dog's head. This does provide you with a better measure of control over your English Cocker Spaniel, but admittedly is still not quite as effective as the flat collar. You will also have to keep the leash short as the dog can become entangled in it if it's too long.

6. Tightening harnesses. Like the ordinary front clip harness, these have the leash attachment in the front rather than on the dog's back. However, they do allow you to cause a slight measure of discomfort to your English Cocker Spaniel if it is not obeying when you pull on the leash and tighten the harness. While this is obviously not as nasty an apparatus as prong or choke collars, remember that you are still dealing with your companion, and so tightening the harness is probably simply overkill for your English Cocker Spaniel.

Don't Expect Miracles and You Won't Be Disappointed

While it is completely true that the great majority of English Cocker Spaniels can be trained to obedience to one degree or another, there are also times when the owner is disappointed in the results, or lack thereof.

Part of the problem could lie in unrealistic expectations. Before you get an English Cocker Spaniel, analyze what you want out of a dog – do you want a dog that will just be content to buddy around within the house and yard, or do you want an active dog that will participate with you in outdoor activities, or are you looking for an active guardian of the home and property? These are important questions because no amount of training will be able to overcome the basic breed characteristics.

6th Chapter: Clicker Training

It may surprise you to learn that clicker training and the concept behind it had its beginnings about 60 years ago. Clicker training is based on conditioning principles that teach the dog to associate the desired behavior with a sound and a treat. The idea is that by using a distinguishing sound, different from human voices or the ordinary background noise, it would help to train any dog, including English Cocker Spaniels, more quickly and efficiently. Other noisemakers, such as whistles, were also contemplated, but the ease and simplicity of using a clicker has made this object the best choice.

When this form of conditioning was first proposed (actually by B.F. Skinner, and others investigating the conditioning process in both humans and animals), it was decided that praising the dog for doing something right with verbal praise or by petting, was too slow to provide an accurate reinforcement; the dog might have trouble understanding that the praise was relevant to the correct behavior. The distinctive 'click' is quick and easy to produce, and for this reason was considered to be superior.

It doesn't matter whether you are starting training with a new English Cocker Spaniel puppy or teaching an old dog new tricks, clicker training could well be the easiest and least stressful way to train your dog for both of you. You will hardly need a pile of expensive equipment, either – all you need is a clicker, treats, and a leash. Some more sensitive English Cocker Spaniels, especially puppies, can be startled by the strong sound the clicker produces; most will get used to the sound quickly, but if you find that your English Cocker Spaniel jumps every time you use the clicker, try substituting a retractable pen; the clicking sound that a pen produces is much softer than that of the clicker, but still distinctive.

Getting Started

The first step in clicker training is to get your English Cocker Spaniel to associate the click with the reward – the treat. At this point, you will not be trying to train your English Cocker Spaniel to sit, stay, or come, but merely to condition your English Cocker Spaniel to realize that after a click is heard, a treat will be forthcoming. You can and should do this in different places of your home and yard, to accustom your English Cocker Spaniel puppy or adult to recognizing the clicker wherever you are. You can even do this stage of the training while sitting watching your favorite television show in the evening.

Begin this initial stage with a good supply of treats (small pieces of something your English Cocker Spaniel particularly likes will work best – remember, you aren't actually feeding your English Cocker Spaniel now). If possible, start this when it's been a few hours since your English Cocker Spaniel adult or puppy has been fed; it will be much keener to get the treats than it will be when its stomach is full. As with all dog training exercises, you will need to repeat this multiple times, but this learned association will lay the foundation for all of your future clicker training.

Don't overdo the repetitions, click and treat a maximum of 10 or 12 times, say, and then let your English Cocker Spaniel relax and get up onto your lap; you can even do the click and treat while your English Cocker Spaniel is snuggled up with you. Vary the time between the clicks, also, making some following on the heels of the previous click, but letting a minute or more go by before the next. Be sure to praise your English Cocker Spaniel after the training session is over. Initial clicker training will be most effective and enjoyable for both of you if you have numerous short lessons throughout the day, rather than 1 or 2 long ones. The attention span of most English Cocker Spaniel puppies and dogs is not overly long, and once the animal becomes bored the lesson will lose its meaning. Sessions of 10 minutes or so are best.

Using Clicker Training

How effective you are with clicker training at this point will depend on your ability to react quickly to what your English Cocker Spaniel is doing. The same basic techniques that you would ordinarily use for basic obedience training can easily be incorporated with clicker use. For example, when you have successfully gotten your English Cocker Spaniel into the "Sit" position, click and give the English Cocker Spaniel a treat.

Make sure you act quickly; the lesson will be pointless if you are trying to teach "Sit" but you don't click until your English Cocker Spaniel is in the process of standing up again; there will be no way that your English Cocker Spaniel will be able to associate the click with sitting in this case.

There are considered to be 3 excellent ways to obedience train your English Cocker Spaniel using a clicker and they are termed: catching, luring, and shaping. Active obedience training generally makes use strongly of shaping and luring, while clicker training makes it easy to add catching to the mix.

1. Catching might well be referred to as "Caught in the act." In this case, it will mean catching your English Cocker Spaniel already doing what you want it to do. If you are trying to teach sit, give the command, then click and treat immediately when you see your English Cocker Spaniel adult or puppy already sitting. Catching can be used for nearly any behavior you are trying to teach, such as "Come" or "Down". Rely on your English Cocker Spaniel's normal activities to teach the behavior you want.

2. Teaching your English Cocker Spaniel to lie down using basic obedience training often involves using a treat to get your English Cocker Spaniel to lower itself to the floor. Dogs tend to resist going down because it puts them in a vulnerable position and they instinctively avoid this. Clicker training can make this somewhat difficult technique easier for your English Cocker

Spaniel to learn. This method is called luring because you are using a lure, the treat, to get your dog to do what you wish. You will be following the same basic clicker idea here as you used with catching, saying "Down", and using a treat to get the animal to lie down, this time, however, you will be adding the click as soon as your English Cocker Spaniel is on the floor, to be followed by the treat.

3. Shaping is used when more complex behaviors might be wanted. Rather than using the click and treat to reward an obvious behavior such as sitting, in this instance you will use your clicker to teach your English Cocker Spaniel a varying number of small steps to attain an ultimate goal. If you want your English Cocker Spaniel to be able to sit up on its hind legs and then offer its paw to be shaken, you will have to teach it first to sit, then to sit up, and finally to stick out its paw. Each step of the process will have to be taught before the next step is undertaken, which can make this a somewhat lengthy process, depending on what exactly is involved. Luring has been used to teach complex activities to service dogs such as putting clothes into a washing machine, taking them out, putting them in the dryer, and then putting the dried clothes into the clothes basket.

Clicker Training to Correct Unwanted English Cocker Spaniel Behavior

Inappropriate behavior by your English Cocker Spaniel adult or puppy can be easier to correct when you use clicker training. Make certain that your English Cocker Spaniel completely understands the connection between the click and the treat before you begin. The sharp sound of the clicker draws your English Cocker Spaniel's attention and makes it easier for it to focus on the task at hand. You will not be using the clicker when your English Cocker Spaniel is engaged in inappropriate behavior (you will, of course, have to intervene with as little fuss as possible if it is chewing on an electric cord or destroying your favorite pair of shoes). In these cases, remove the object from the English Cocker Spaniel without saying anything, or simply saying "No!", and then try offering a chew toy instead. If your English Cocker Spaniel begins chewing the toy, click and treat.

Although it will take some time, your English Cocker Spaniel will eventually learn to direct itself to approved behavior in order to hear the click and receive a treat. By responding to the positive reinforcement of the clicker signals, your dog will gradually unlearn the bad behavior. This will take time and patience on your part, so be prepared to stay calm and persistent throughout the 'unlearning' process. Keep in mind that the longer you have allowed negative behavior to continue, the longer it will take to correct.

7th Chapter: Teaching Tricks

English Cocker Spaniels are intelligent dogs and are able to learn a wide range of tricks. Teaching your English Cocker Spaniel tricks is not only a way to provide for a more amusing companion, but also a way for you and your English Cocker Spaniel to bond more closely together. As with almost anything you are trying to teach your English Cocker Spaniel, it is always important to use patience and positive reinforcements to achieve the best results. Dogs in general try to please their owners, and this is even more evident in dogs that are used exclusively as companions.

You will probably find that the best results when teaching your English Cocker Spaniel tricks will be to use a clicker. If you haven't used clicker training before, please read the section in this book that deals with this. Once you and your English Cocker Spaniel have the basic clicker principals understood, you'll be ready to start teaching tricks to your English Cocker Spaniel. While there are obviously dozens of tricks that you can teach to your English Cocker Spaniel, it's probably best to start with a few simple ones, then move onto more complicated tricks. Your English Cocker Spaniel should also be obedience trained before you even consider teaching tricks to it, so if you haven't done this yet, backtrack and take care of that first; many of the tricks will be built on basic obedience commands.

1. "Shake". This is the old reliable trick and is one of the easiest to learn, as your English Cocker Spaniel probably already has a tendency to give you the 'paw of friendship'. Get your English Cocker Spaniel to sit, then hold a treat just out of reach. If your English Cocker Spaniel gets up to get the treat, return it to the sit position. Most dogs will start to paw at the air in order to get the treat, and this is precisely when you should click if you are using a clicker, say "Shake" and give the dog the treat. As this is

a natural action on your English Cocker Spaniel's part to begin with, "Shake" will undoubtedly be simple to teach, and it won't be long before your English Cocker Spaniel is offering its paw on command.

2. "Roll over". Your English Cocker Spaniel must know the 'down' command in order to learn this trick. After putting your English Cocker Spaniel into the down position, hold a treat in front of its nose then move it to one side or the other. If your English Cocker Spaniel gets up, tell it 'down' again. In time you will be able to get your English Cocker Spaniel to roll over onto its side. Treat and praise immediately once this step has been done. The more difficult step will be to get your English Cocker Spaniel to roll over onto its back, but repetition will accomplish this in time.

3. "Push". I've taught my dogs this so that they can get into the house easily during cold weather; sometimes I'll be waiting outside for one to finish its business while the other is already done. Leave the door nearly closed, and encourage your English Cocker Spaniel to get as near to it as possible. Once your English Cocker Spaniel's head touches the door, say "Push, push". Don't hesitate to help your English Cocker Spaniel along by giving a gentle shove while giving the command. Some English Cocker Spaniels might be a bit hesitant to push against the door, but should come over fairly quickly.

4. "Pull". You can also teach your English Cocker Spaniel to open doors. The key to learning this trick is to attach a cloth to the handle of the door; this will give your English Cocker Spaniel something it can get a hold of. This trick will be easier to teach if you have already played tug of war with your English Cocker Spaniel. If you have not done so, start out by doing this, and when your English Cocker Spaniel tugs on the cloth or rope, say "Pull". It shouldn't be too difficult to get your English Cocker Spaniel to tug on the rope or cloth that you attach to a door. You

might want to be careful about putting a cloth on the refrigerator door, however.

5. "Take". All dogs have a prey drive, and it's obvious that this instinct is still a part of their nature. Put a toy down on the floor near your English Cocker Spaniel and as soon as it grabs the toy, click and say "Take". Provide a treat and praise, and soon your English Cocker Spaniel will pick up a nearby object upon your command.

6. "Bring". The flipside to the 'take' command is 'bring'. Once your English Cocker Spaniel has picked up the toy or other object on your 'take' command, you will want to teach it to bring it to you. You probably won't get your English Cocker Spaniel to bring the toy to you the first time, so use increments to achieve this trick. Tell your English Cocker Spaniel to "Bring", and if it takes even one step towards you, click and treat. It won't take too long for your pup to associate moving towards you with the toy with the command and a treat. Be sure to be lavish with praise once your English Cocker Spaniel delivers the toy to you.

7. Bringing specific objects. In addition to bringing a toy to you, your English Cocker Spaniel can also be taught to bring specific objects. Yes, your English Cocker Spaniel can be taught to bring you your slippers or the newspaper or any other thing that this dog can reach and handle. Those who require a cane to walk can teach their English Cocker Spaniel to bring that to them. The first step will be teaching the English Cocker Spaniel to associate the object with the word, and once that has been accomplished, you will have to combine that with 'take' and 'bring'.

As with nearly all forms of dog training, your English Cocker Spaniel will do best if you use positive reinforcement exclusively for teaching tricks. And remember, once you or your English Cocker Spaniel start to get frustrated, irritable, or lose patience, stop training immediately and do something pleasant together.

8th Chapter: Training the Difficult English Cocker Spaniel

Living with a difficult English Cocker Spaniel is akin to living with a problematic human family member – life can be extremely difficult and uncomfortable for all concerned. Difficulty with English Cocker Spaniels can take several forms: aggression to people or pets, problem barking, soiling the house, hyperactivity, and destruction of property. Some, if not most, of these problems can be overcome with persistence and training. It is best to never ignore your English Cocker Spaniel as this can lead to it exhibiting aggressive or other undesirable behavior, and this can make living with them a hellish existence.

People who have English Cocker Spaniels that are exhibiting behavioral problems are often the cause of these problems. Very often people choose the wrong dog for their lifestyle, or fail to train it properly. Some breeds are simply harder to train than others, and this can include English Cocker Spaniels.

You should also recognize that some dogs can also come with inborn behavioral problems that no amount of training can fix (often the result of inbreeding by irresponsible breeders in most cases). When dealing with a difficult English Cocker Spaniel, you have to realize that whatever problems exist (and there can be multiple difficulties) will take time, patience, and often money to correct if you want to have a pleasant household companion.

It is also true that some English Cocker Spaniels (like other breeds of dog) are mentally deficient in one way or another – like people, English Cocker Spaniels can be born with mental disorders that will be impossible to correct. Other dogs can just be, well, stupid. Depending on the nature of the mental state that is interfering with training, some English Cocker Spaniels, even those that are slower than the average, and seemingly impossible to train, can still make good and loving companions.

As with most training in regard to dogs, not only is the breed of dog that you choose important, but the age at which you get the dog is equally important. The best time to get an English Cocker Spaniel puppy is between 7 and 12 weeks of age. At this point, the puppy has learned the basics of pecking order from its mother and siblings, and will be at the perfect age to adjust to living in a human household and bond with you. Puppies younger than this often exhibit training problems later, simply because they have missed out on this important 'natural training', and juvenile or adult English Cocker Spaniels that are brought into the home when they are over 3 or 4 months old (if they have just been confined to a kennel without much human contact) may always exhibit a wild dog mentality, and they will be unable to be trained at all.

A neighbor got a puppy when it was 8 months old. Prior to this, the dog had been kept in a small pen where it was able to watch its mother chase cars and trucks every day. Not only this, but the breeder spent literally no time with the dog at all, it had no contact with humans. This was the behavior that the dog learned, and although my neighbor tried literally for months to train the dog not to chase vehicles, it was impossible to break the habit. The last straw was when it actually attacked a car, biting at the tires and throwing itself at the car's windows to try to get to the people inside. After that, the dog was kept on an airline cable to give it plenty of room to run, but an inability to reach the road. This dog was never comfortable inside the home and always wanted to get outside, and exhibited on-again-off-again aggression towards the owners. Rather than offload the dog onto someone else, however, or have it put down, they did give it as much freedom as possible, as well as taking care of its physical needs. This dog never wanted to spend much time with people at all, and if free would range literally miles from the home, leaving its signature hole with a rock in it to mark the extent of its travels.

English Cocker Spaniels with a wild dog mentality find it very difficult to bond with people. This is not the dog's fault, it is the fault of the breeders, but the wild dog syndrome is nearly impossible to overcome – the die is cast. An English Cocker Spaniel with wild dog syndrome can still be a fairly decent pet, however, the instincts of the breed are to be companionable with humans, so as long as you keep strict controls over your English Cocker Spaniel, especially when it is outside the home, chances are that you and your English Cocker Spaniel will be able to get through life together.

Is There a Solution?

If you have chosen an English Cocker Spaniel, and for whatever reason, you are unable to train it, and it fails to live up to your expectations, you will eventually have to make some decisions, based on a number of factors.

1. The nature of the training problem will play a large part. An English Cocker Spaniel that simply cannot or will not learn basic obedience commands, but that is otherwise a fairly well-behaved dog that gets along with the family will not present as thorny a problem as a dog that growls, snarls, or bites. Aggression towards people or other pets is dangerous and cannot be tolerated.

2. The size of the dog is also important – for example, a small dog in comparison to a larger dog would pose less of a threat. Either way, children will have to be kept away from an English Cocker Spaniel with aggression problems, and should never be left alone with it under any circumstances.

3. Are you willing and able to devote more of your time to intensively trying to train your English Cocker Spaniel? Most of us, unfortunately, have little free time available, so unless you

do have the time and patience to devote to training your English Cocker Spaniel, you may simply have to give up on training. Training a difficult English Cocker Spaniel can take weeks or months, although English Cocker Spaniels and other dogs with behavior problems can often become valued pets, the big question is whether you have the time and patience to do so.

4. Animal behaviorists can often help with any kind of training problem. This can range from housetraining to obedience to agility, and whether you come to rely upon one for helping with your English Cocker Spaniel will depend not only on the problem behavior, but also on how dedicated you are to training the dog. If your English Cocker Spaniel is consistently exhibiting aggression, however, you should consult an animal behaviorist. You can still be sued if your English Cocker Spaniel bites a visitor and a passerby on the street. However, animal behaviorists do not offer their services free of charge, and using one of these specialists can cost quite a bit of money. The possibility that you might have to rely on an animal behaviorist to cure your English Cocker Spaniel of serious behavioral problems, and the cost of this treatment, should also be taken into consideration. Will you be able to afford it?

Those who feel that the English Cocker Spaniel's training problems, while perhaps insurmountable, are something that can be accepted and lived with, will likely keep their dog and come to terms with its behavior. The real sticking point will be where the dog's behavior is overly aggressive. If your English Cocker Spaniel has bitten you or anyone else, a consultation with your veterinarian is essential, not only to rule out disease or injury, but also to advise you on the best course to take. A bite, even one that is not serious, should be seen by a doctor as soon as possible, to lessen the chances of infection.

9th Chapter: Behavioral Training

All of us hope, when we get an English Cocker Spaniel adult or puppy, that it will turn out to be the perfect pet of which we were dreaming. Unfortunately, just as the behavior of human beings often leaves a great deal to be desired, so can the behavior of the canines we bring into our homes. Adverse behavior can cause us to become angry, frustrated, and can lead to the pet being consigned to a rescue group or placed in a shelter, often to be euthanized. Before these steps are taken, however, behavior training might be the answer to the problem.

Behavioral training can be looked upon as the training that must be done when obedience training has either failed or has not been done in the first place, and can, in many cases be corrected.

In most cases, poor behavior on the part of the English Cocker Spaniel can be traced to poor training, or no training, while the dog was young, and as long as the English Cocker Spaniel is mentally sound, and you have the time and patience to curb the inappropriate behavior, you can often wind up with a well-behaved dog. However, in some cases, abuse while the dog was young, or poor breeding practices will make behavioral training difficult or impossible. Owners will sometimes come up against an English Cocker Spaniel that is simply mentally defective in one way or another that will make instituting proper behavior impossible.

The fad for "line breeding" has often resulted in dogs that may meet a physical standard for conformation, but that have lost the mental traits often associated with the breed. For example, there are a range of breeds that became notable for their extreme good nature, but because some breeders bred siblings and cousins together, or even bred parents to their offspring, conditions such as 'sudden rage syndrome' now afflicts them.

Dogs that are subject to sudden rage syndrome (idiopathic rage, over-aggression) are not responsible for their actions and are unable to control them when the aggression is triggered – sometimes there is no trigger at all, there is just a suddenly launched attack on whoever is unlucky enough to be near the dog. The sad thing is that their genetic makeup is defective, and at this point in time cannot be corrected. Some vets will prescribe medication to try to control this behavior, but the results have been mixed. Some have likened sudden rage syndrome to epilepsy, especially as the dog has absolutely no control over it.

Fortunately, most adverse behaviors that English Cocker Spaniels exhibit will respond well to behavioral training, and can help reform a dog that has proven itself to be a pest into a valuable and cherished family member. When using behavioral training, once again the focus will be on positive reinforcement, although verbal remonstrance may be necessary in some cases; avoid screaming, if you have to correct the English Cocker Spaniel verbally, say "No!" in a firm voice, rather than ranting at the dog. Once again, too, patience and understanding will be required; anger and frustration have no place in behavioral training.

Before trying to actively correct unwanted behavior in your English Cocker Spaniel, use obedience training to teach the basics of 'sit', 'stay', 'come', and 'down'. Once your English Cocker Spaniel has mastered these basic commands it will be ready to undertake the more difficult task of undoing problem behavior, and you will be much more likely to correct the behavior quickly and successfully. Regardless of what trainers who say that leadership training is wrong, simply by training your dog to obedience, you are being the leader; the dog is taking instructions from you, period. You can be a kind leader, there is nothing in the world to contradict that, and by being so you will not only help your dog overcome its problems, and give it more confidence, but will also establish that important bond between you.

Barking

Problem barking not only is irritating to you and the members of your household; it is also very irritating to your neighbors. Consider it the equivalent of having someone blaring music that you despised out of their house or apartment for hours at a time; having a problem barker can create social problems for you, and some people have even been sued because of the noise their dog was making. At the very best, if you allow your English Cocker Spaniel to continue to bark and disturb the neighbors you are inconsiderate, and at the very worst, you could be subject to an enormous legal judgment against you, or by having an irate neighbor react harshly towards your dog. It has been known for dogs to have been poisoned or killed by neighbors at the end of their rope due to incessant barking.

Some owners seem to have a shut off valve in their ears that keeps them from being bothered by incessant barking, but others are just as annoyed as their neighbors might be. There are some measures you can take to help keep problem barking from starting in the first place, and to curb it if it does develop later.

Barking is a natural behavior to an English Cocker Spaniel and is one of the ways that the animal communicates. However, be aware of this as you could find yourself with an English Cocker Spaniel with a big mouth that barks excessively. Barking can be used to give a warning when a stranger approaches, an English Cocker Spaniel might bark from joy when its master returns, dogs sometimes bark while playing, and some English Cocker Spaniels just seem to bark for the sake of hearing their own voice; these dogs will often bark when they are lonely or bored or afraid.

The first step to stopping problem barking is to determine exactly why your English Cocker Spaniel is barking. If it is barking only when it's been left tied out in the yard by itself, the obvious solution is to bring the animal inside. However, most excessive barking will require a bit more work to overcome. As with most training, it will take effort and time on your part, but you will be rewarded with a quieter and more pleasant companion, and one that is less likely to get you dragged into court. English Cocker Spaniels with separation anxiety will also often bark excessively, and this problem will be handled later in this section. There are some steps you can take to curb problem barking:

1. Do not yell at the English Cocker Spaniel to try to get it to stop barking, it will probably think you are joining in the fun.

2. If people walking by on the street are instigating barking while the dog is in the home, close the curtains. Barking at people when outside should also be discouraged – take the dog inside at once.

3. Reward quiet and ignore barking. This one can be difficult because it's hard for anyone to listen to a dog barking for hours without reacting. However, if you can bear it, wait until your English Cocker Spaniel stops barking and then reward with a treat and praise. Needless to say, this approach might take some time, and will also require some forbearing neighbors, as well as nerves of steel on your part. However, do not expect neighbors to tolerate this form of training indefinitely, at some point, they will complain again or call authorities.

4. If your English Cocker Spaniel barks at other dogs, you can also help it to become 'numb' to other dogs by enlisting the help of a friend. This person should stand out of sight with his or her dog. You should have your English Cocker Spaniel on leash. Make sure you have plenty of treats on hand and start giving them to your English Cocker Spaniel even before your friend and the other dog makes an appearance. Once your friend shows up, stop giving treats when the English Cocker Spaniel barks, but once it stops give the dog a treat. This technique will require quite a few repeats, as you can imagine.

5. When your English Cocker Spaniel is barking, request that it be "Quiet" in a normal voice. Repeat the command until your English Cocker Spaniel stops barking, even for a brief moment. As soon as the barking stops treat your English Cocker Spaniel and say "Quiet". Eventually it will understand that a treat will be forthcoming if it stops barking.

6. Some English Cocker Spaniels will bark because they have failed to receive the stimulation and exercise that they require every day. Giving these dogs the exercise they need can often eliminate the barking problem.

7. Various types of collars are sometimes used to control barking. Collars that spray citronella have been effective for some problem barkers. Shock collars are controversial – a woman I knew had to choose between getting rid of a problem barker and using a shock collar and did try the collar. She reported that the dog needed only one shock before it learned not to bark. However, few people have as good a result using shock collars and the dog often ends up with a damaged throat unless the collar is used properly and only for a short period of time. As noted previously, English Cocker Spaniels can easily ignore pain, so using a shock collar to control barking will probably be a waste of money.

Surgery to remove your English Cocker Spaniel's voice box, debarking, is even more controversial than shock collars. This is probably better than having the English Cocker Spaniel euthanized, but not much. Some dogs experience constant postoperative pain or have a greater chance of choking. And, like tonsils, some voice boxes will grow back, and the problem barking will start right up again.

Aggression and Biting

Aggression and biting are what are responsible (in addition to soiling the house) for causing the greatest number of dogs of any breed to be surrendered to shelters. These behaviors are completely unacceptable in a companion dog and must be curbed immediately. Although the theory of the human being the 'pack leader' has come under a cloud in some quarters of late, there is simply no denying that when the English Cocker Spaniel looks up to the humans in the household, and considers that they are of a higher standing than it is, that there will be much less possibility of biting or aggression.

Being the 'alpha' in the home doesn't mean that the human is going to be punishing the dog constantly to keep it submissive. It means that the animal understands that the human is the ultimate arbiter. Any situation where the human is telling the dog what to do, or otherwise directing the dog's actions automatically places the human in the superior position; and this includes obedience training. As Dick Deadeye says in Gilbert and Sullivan's light opera Pinafore, "When people have to follow other people's orders, equality is out of the question." And this pertains to people and dogs too.

When we brought our first English Cocker Spaniel home, she voluntarily exhibited submissive behavior to my eldest son. As soon as she saw my son, she instantly lowered herself to her stomach and crept up to him. When she reached him, she flipped over onto her side and exposed her belly. My son had done nothing to make her feel submissive – in fact all of us went out of our way to make her feel welcome and comfortable. This was instinctive behavior on her part. English Cocker Spaniels do not necessarily feel that we are 'dominating' them in any way by training them, or as can be seen with our first English Cocker Spaniel, just by being there, they simply accept this as being normal.

In most cases, aggression and biting will never arise with your English Cocker Spaniel adult or puppy, especially if you begin training a new puppy as soon as it comes into the home. Fortunately, most English Cocker Spaniels have an agreeable and balanced disposition, and the need for behavior control as regards to biting will never arise. However, it can happen and understanding how to deal with it is important for both you and your pet.

What might be considered 'normal aggression' in an English Cocker Spaniel will usually begin with barking, which is a warning to you to back off now. If you ignore the warning, it will progress to growling, then snarling, where the teeth are exposed, and if you proceed with what you are doing, the English Cocker Spaniel will probably bite. A bite in this case will usually be 'light' often not even breaking the skin, but it is still a bite. Even a very small dog can inflict a serious bite.

An English Cocker Spaniel can deliver a very painful bite and this could very quickly lead to an infection. An adult English Cocker Spaniel that suddenly starts biting must be taken to the veterinarian as soon as possible to rule out any physical illness or injury that might be causing this behavior. If your English Cocker Spaniel checks out, and has no physical problems, then ask your vet to recommend an animal behaviorist – biting is too serious a matter for you to undertake correcting yourself; you could be injured if you attempt to correct your English Cocker Spaniel.

If your English Cocker Spaniel puppy begins to show aggression, it's possible to stop this before it becomes ingrained behavior, but it must be addressed immediately when the problem manifests itself. All puppies use mouthing as a form of play and communication. Under natural conditions, when puppies are engaged in play and one of them goes too far, the injured pup will squeal, and this causes the biter to back off. When this happens with you, you can substitute a rather loud "No!" or "Stop!" in the place of the squeal. The sooner you begin doing this, the less likely it is that your puppy will continue biting you. Do not strike the puppy, usually a sharp verbal reprimand will be sufficient. Most English Cocker Spaniel puppies will really take such a reprimand to heart, and if you notice that your pup's feelings seem to have been hurt, do not try to comfort it, it understands that it has misbehaved and will come out of its funk on its own. If you comfort the puppy at this point, you will only be encouraging future bites.

In addition to verbally reprimanding your puppy, make sure that you have plenty of safe toys and chews on hand; if you notice the puppy starting to zero in on your fingers or hand, place a chew in the way. The idea of biting your hand will eventually fade from your puppy's mind as it comes to associate a toy or chew with using its teeth.

English Cocker Spaniel puppies and dogs will exhibit possession over food and other resources (including toys, humans, and furniture), just as other dogs do. This is normal and natural to an extent as wild canids do have to protect their food from theft, but it has no place in the human home.

As soon as your puppy enters your home, begin training it to accept that you can take its food dish away if you wish, and can also take food, or other things, out of its mouth without any resistance. We have always done this with our dogs and have never had a problem with food aggression with any of them. They also take food from our hands in a gentle manner, rather than swallowing our hand up to the wrist.

1. Put your English Cocker Spaniel puppy's dish in front of it and then take it away. If your puppy does not react in any way, reward it by returning the dish and praising your puppy. If your puppy growls, say "No!" in a loud voice and do not return the dish right away.

Repeat this over and over until even the most possessive puppy comes to accept that you have the right to its food whenever you want. This right should extend to every member of the human family, also; every human in the household has to be 'above' the dog in the family social order.

2. Your puppy must learn to accept that you can stick your hand in its mouth to remove food or any other object whenever you wish. Hand your puppy a treat and then take it out of the pup's mouth. Most English Cocker Spaniel puppies will simply accept this without demur, although some will need the same kind of training that is used with the food dish.

3. Never strike the puppy or intimidate it over this issue – if it won't cooperate on its own or with a simple "No!" command, physical force is not going to work, either, it will probably only exacerbate the problem and make the young dog afraid of you. Fear is at the root of many biting problems, so you do not want to make your pup afraid of you.

4. If your English Cocker Spaniel puppy persists in biting you, consult your veterinarian immediately. A puppy should be responsive to your authority. Continued biting will only get worse as the puppy reaches adulthood, it will not get better.

Even the games that you play with your puppy can cause it to become more aggressive and more likely to bite you or others. Tug-of-war can also develop problematic behavior, so skip this activity with your English Cocker Spaniel puppy. Once again, we never had any problems with this with our dogs. Providing sufficient exercise and play opportunities for your puppy can help to prevent biting from occurring in the first place.

Biting and nipping can also occur while the puppy is teething. Providing toys, nylon bones, and chew hooves when the pup is cutting teeth can help to direct them to acceptable chewing objects. If you are nipped, say "No!" and make a chewing toy available, praising when the puppy chews on that. Puppies will also be more likely to nip when they become overexcited while playing; keeping play times a bit shorter can help keep your puppy from reaching the nipping stage. Always remember to never leave a strong-jawed puppy alone with rawhide chews – the puppy might bite off a large piece and swallow it, resulting either in choking or intestinal blockage.

Aggression can also be manifested by your English Cocker Spaniel adult or puppy denying you access to your couch, chair, or even bed. Don't let your puppy get away with this at all. It's fairly easy to remove a puppy from your furniture with a stern "No!" if you respond to the aggression instantly. Letting your puppy up on your furniture is up to you (we have always allowed it), but if you do allow it, make sure that your puppy realizes that it's a place to share. Don't hesitate, however, to reinforce good behavior with your puppy; give the pup treats and praise it when it behaves well, especially if it is already in possession and you move in with no problem. If you decide not to allow your English Cocker Spaniel up on the furniture, make certain that it has comfortable pillows or beds available at various points in the home.

Biting in an adult dog is a serious and potentially dangerous problem. You, family members, other people, and other pets are all in danger from a biting dog. Thousands of serious bites are delivered every year by dogs, and fatalities also occur. A bite from even a small dog can be damaging and the wound could go septic. You should never consider that you are capable of correcting this problem safely by yourself, but must always seek professional assistance when attempting to deal with biting.

Car Chasing

To many dogs, a passing car or truck (or even a person or someone cycling) is prey to chase after, and this could include your English Cocker Spaniel. All dogs have a prey drive to one degree or another, but it will be stronger in some breeds than in others. You might well have a dog that is totally blasé about cars or an easily excitable dog that cannot resist chasing them. Some dogs couldn't care a fig about traffic and will have no interest in chasing vehicles, while others will go after anything on wheels, including bicycles, scooters, and skate boards. Although an English Cocker Spaniel should never be allowed to run freely outside in a densely populated area, there are times when this may happen. Remember as well that English Cocker Spaniels will have a natural instinct that is present within them that should be recognized.

Car chasing is extremely dangerous for your English Cocker Spaniel; as it can easily be injured or killed by a vehicle. Even if your English Cocker Spaniel is not killed, serious injury will mean that you will have to take it to the veterinarian for expensive care. Veterinary care can be nearly as expensive as human medical care, and a seriously injured English Cocker Spaniel can easily rack up a number of costs in veterinary bills within a short period of time, especially if surgery is required to save your English Cocker Spaniel's life. In addition to the direct cost to you and your English Cocker Spaniel, you could also be liable for costs associated with an accident. Laws do vary from country to country, but in most cases, you can be sued if your dog causes a vehicular accident.

Many dogs are not simply content to chase after a vehicle, either, they will attack it. It's not uncommon for aggressive dogs to try to bite the tires or even jump onto the hood of a car – as can be seen from the behavior of my friend's puppy, described previously. This compounds the danger for the driver as well as for the dog.

Of course, the most logical and intelligent thing to do is to prevent car chasing from becoming a problem in the first place. Responsible owners do not open the door and let their English Cocker Spaniels out to 'do their thing' for the day, letting them back in at night to eat and sleep. Once you have decided that you are going to own an English Cocker Spaniel, you are responsible for every minute of the animal's life – if you are unable to accept this responsibility, you should not own a dog of any kind.

Most states in America require that you have your dog leashed when it is outside with you. This will help to prevent car chasing from becoming a problem at all. If leashing is not required, then the owner should always be present with the dog when it's outside.

For those people whose English Cocker Spaniels have begun to show an interest in passing traffic, but have not yet begun to actively chase cars, there are several things that you can do to help prevent acceleration of the problem:

1. If car chasing has not actually begun, you can often redirect your English Cocker Spaniel's attention. You will have to stand with your English Cocker Spaniel, securely leashed, near the road. Whenever a car appears, distract your English Cocker Spaniel with a treat, and praise it when it turns its attention to the treat.

2. Electric fencing cannot be relied upon to control your English Cocker Spaniel's behavior; these dogs can often just ignore the discomfort and run right through the signal to chase the vehicle.

3. Reinforce obedience training in the home, the yard, and near the road. Make sure that you treat and praise every time your English Cocker Spaniel obeys you and resists attempting to chase cars.

4. Keeping your English Cocker Spaniel properly exercised (tired out) will also help keep it out of the road; a dog that has just returned from a long walk and intensive play session will be more likely to ignore traffic.

If your English Cocker Spaniel is already chasing cars, there are a few things you can try, but ultimately you may have to seek the help of an animal behaviorist. Having someone throw water balloons at your English Cocker Spaniel while driving past, turning your hose on your English Cocker Spaniel, or using a noxious smelling spray only demonstrates that the problem is already beyond your control and you need professional help to deal with it. You should also examine how you are controlling your English Cocker Spaniel in the first place – should this dog be outside without supervision.

The behavior of your English Cocker Spaniel ultimately reflects on you, both morally and legally. No dog should be left to wander at will, and when outside should always be under the control of the owner, in a fenced yard, or on a chain (the least desirable situation, but still better than running free). Leaving your English Cocker Spaniel outside on its own is hardly a wise thing to do under any circumstances.

Separation Anxiety

Our English Cocker Spaniels have always exhibited a high degree of separation anxiety, when away from us for even short periods of time. When our first English Cocker Spaniel had to have dental work done she banged her head against the cage afterwards to such a degree that there were bumps and cuts on it. I even called the vet back the next day to ask about the damage and this was when they told me about her behavior. When she had to be hospitalized for a serious illness, the vet had to take her out of the cage and let her wander through the office so that she wouldn't harm herself. She also refused to eat at all, and only took a little water. We are fortunate in being at home constantly, and our constant presence has solved the problem for us, but others, who must be out of the home during the day, will need to find another solution.

Separation anxiety differs from simply inappropriate behavior because it only happens when you are out of the house. A badly trained English Cocker Spaniel will soil the house right in front of you, while an English Cocker Spaniel with separation anxiety will only do so when you are absent. Never punish your English Cocker Spaniel for any messes it may have made in your absence; it will have no idea why you are scolding or hitting it -- the deed is long done. Finding a way for your English Cocker Spaniel to deal with separation anxiety is the intelligent and humane answer.

There are several theories on why one dog will develop separation anxiety and another will be able to tolerate owner absences without a problem. The breed of the dog will have some bearing on this subject; many dog breeds, like the English Cocker Spaniel, have developed to act as companions to humans, but any dog, of any breed can suffer from separation anxiety. Another factor in this condition appears to be that English Cocker Spaniels that have suffered an upset in their lives -- such as being returned to the kennel in which they were bred (often due to the breakup of their human family), or dogs that have been placed in shelters – will be more likely to exhibit anxiety when left alone. These English Cocker Spaniels undoubtedly fear that they will be dumped somewhere again, and because of their strong attachment to their new owners, are particularly liable to exhibit separation anxiety.

Dealing with separation anxiety to the extent that your English Cocker Spaniel can comfortably and safely be left alone can be difficult, but it can be done in most cases.

1. Do not make a big production out of leaving the house; leave without even bidding the dog good-bye. English Cocker Spaniels with separation anxiety will quickly pick up on cues that you are getting ready to leave (picking up your purse, dressing in 'going out' clothing, shrugging on your coat). Minimize these cues as much as you are able, and also perform these activities at random times so that the dog does not automatically associate them with your leaving. For example, pick up your purse before

dinner and then sit down to eat with it, or change your clothes before watching television.

2. Try to make a spot in the home where your English Cocker Spaniel feels comfortable and safe while you're out. If your English Cocker Spaniel likes being in its crate, you can use this, otherwise a specific room will do. If your English Cocker Spaniel hates being in a crate, do not put your English Cocker Spaniel into it while you are out, it will only make it more fearful and also likely to injure itself in its desperation to get out.

3. You can cut back on the amount of attention and affection that you give your English Cocker Spaniel so that, frankly, it just doesn't like you as much as it did before and doesn't care if you go out. Personally, I feel that this is a completely wrong approach and defeats the purpose of having a companion dog in the first place. I consider this to be a solution that borders on the moronic.

4. Use short 'absences' to train your English Cocker Spaniel to accept your absences. Leave the house for only a few seconds, and before your English Cocker Spaniel can begin to misbehave, come back in again. Do not enter if you hear barking or howling or whining, wait until it's become quiet. Gradually lengthen the periods you are away until, hopefully, your English Cocker Spaniel will accept your absence without problem. Don't make a fuss over your English Cocker Spaniel when you enter, however, the point is to keep leaving and entering as uneventful as possible.

5. Some people will ask their veterinarians for tranquilizers for their dog. These should only be looked upon as a stepping stone until you are able to change your English Cocker Spaniel's behavior.

As with all aspects of dog training, trying to modify your English Cocker Spaniel's separation anxiety just might not work out at all; there will always be a small percentage of dogs that are unable to mentally adjust to their owner's absence. There is no really easy solution here for those who have to be out of the home during the day, but English Cocker Spaniels that are unable to overcome separation anxiety can sometimes be left with relatives or friends or even placed in doggy daycare. For those who can do so, you might even take your English Cocker Spaniel to work with you. This will only be possible with a calm English Cocker Spaniel that will be little likely to disrupt the workplace, and is one more reason why it's a good idea to obedience train your English Cocker Spaniel.

Digging

If you have ever gone out into your yard and twisted your ankle on a hole that your English Cocker Spaniel has dug, or found yourself stammering apologies to the neighbor because your English Cocker Spaniel has dug up a prized azalea plant, you understand how frustrating a dog's digging addiction can be. The digging instinct is present in all dogs, and that means that your English Cocker Spaniel could also cause problems with digging.

As with most canine behavior, English Cocker Spaniels dig for a number of reasons; dogs left out in the yard for too long will dig from boredom or to escape; English Cocker Spaniels that feel too hot will dig to provide a nice, cool place to lie down; dogs dig to bury things; and an English Cocker Spaniel might even be mimicking your gardening behavior. English Cocker Spaniels are known to be very good mimics of other creature's behavior, so finding a hole in your lawn could just be a case of your English Cocker Spaniel doing some gardening on its own.

Obviously, the solution to problem digging in most of these cases is simply to keep your English Cocker Spaniel inside unless you are outside with it. Any English Cocker Spaniel left outside on its own is simply a problem in the making in one way or another, even if you have a securely fenced yard or have chained your English Cocker Spaniel.

If, for whatever reason, your English Cocker Spaniel will be spending time outside without a human presence, there are some things that you can do to minimize, if not eliminate, digging. I have driven past yards where dogs were simply left out on their own, and if this will be the case with your English Cocker Spaniel, digging can be eliminated or controlled in a number of ways.

1. Make an area where your English Cocker Spaniel will be allowed to dig to its heart's content. Use stones or a few sticks to mark out the perimeter and then bury some treats or toys in the spot. You will have to monitor your English Cocker Spaniel until it has become accustomed to using this area, and leading your English Cocker Spaniel to the designated area and praising it when digging is done there can help to prevent your yard from becoming an obstacle course and moonscape. Over the course of time, the earth at the designated spot may become thinned out so be sure to add new material when necessary.

2. Exercise can often eliminate the digging problem. Taking your English Cocker Spaniel on a daily walk (as long as it isn't too hot) and playing with it can help to drain off some of that excess energy and leave your English Cocker Spaniel too tired to dig.

3. Spending time teaching your English Cocker Spaniel some tricks can help it feel like it's doing something constructive as well as getting some attention from you.

While digging is not the worst behavior an English Cocker Spaniel can engage in, it certainly can be annoying and can destroy your yard if your English Cocker Spaniel is an especially vigorous digger and you leave it outside unsupervised. The best approach is to analyze why your English Cocker Spaniel is doing it and then find a workable solution – even if this means keeping your English Cocker Spaniel inside with you.

Chewing

Although puppies are undoubtedly the worst when it comes to inappropriate chewing, dogs of any age can cause destruction to your home and belongings. When the 'baby teeth' of puppies begin to break through the gums, and several months later when the adult teeth do so, the pup will have an instinctive drive to chew to relieve the discomfort and help the teeth emerge by chewing on anything it can reach. You may be surprised at how much damage a small puppy can do when teething.

Our puppies, weighing only a couple of pounds, acted like beavers on our wooden dining room chairs. Yes, we gave them chew hooves and toys, but they preferred furniture (they could sometimes be distracted by squeaky toys). We directed them away from the chair legs, but they were persistent and rather cunning and did manage to do some pretty respectable damage to them. However, as soon as the teeth were through, they stopped chewing immediately and have never set tooth to furniture, clothing, or shoes in the following 11 years. We were philosophical about it, tried preventing it as much as possible, and shrugged off the damage.

Puppies, like human babies, also use the mouth as an exploratory tool, and tend to put anything they can between their teeth. An English Cocker Spaniel puppy, after giving a new object a close sniff, will probably grab it with its mouth. Your pup has no concept of the value of any object in your home; everything is simply a potential chew.

However, although most puppy chewing is the result of teething, you should take your puppy to the vet when this behavior begins, to make sure that there isn't a nutritional problem present as well. An upset of the stomach and/or intestinal tract can also cause a puppy (or dog) to chew. Worms can also cause this behavior, so make sure that these are ruled out also.

Most parents discover that the easiest way to get through their toddler's exploratory phase is to 'child-proof' the home. This works well with English Cocker Spaniel puppies, too, and it's probably a good idea to 'puppy-proof' your home when you bring a young dog into it. Removing or protecting objects that might be destroyed or cause harm to the puppy will protect the pup and keep you from getting angry and frustrated: it's a good idea to cover electric cords and remove valuable pieces of furniture until the puppy grows out of its chewing phase.

Giving your puppy something else to chew on can work with some pups, but from my own experience, it will not work every time. Always monitor your English Cocker Spaniel puppy when it is chewing, even if this involves an 'approved' chew. Some puppies have much stronger jaws than you might imagine (ours did) and not only were they able to chew through chair legs, they were also able to completely pull apart toys to get at the squeaker. You should never leave your English Cocker Spaniel adult or puppy alone with a rawhide chew – it's easy for the dog to chew off a piece and swallow it raising the possibility of an intestinal obstruction or choking.

Once the teething stage is over, most puppies will abandon the worst of their chewing behavior. All dogs love to chew to some extent, but dogs that continue destructive chewing after teething are indicating that a larger problem exists.

1. English Cocker Spaniels with separation anxiety often exhibit destructive chewing. Until the basic problem is resolved (see above) the dog will continue to chew and destroy.

2. Dogs that are not receiving the proper amount of exercise are more likely to expend some of their spare energy by chewing. Make sure that you give your chewing English Cocker Spaniel a long walk every day (except when it's too hot), and take the time to play with it, too; English Cocker Spaniels that are tired

and have worked out their energy will be less likely to chew inappropriately.

3. Dogs that are bored will simply chew for something to do. Even a dog whose main reason in life is to be a companion will become bored without some kind of stimulation. In addition to providing enough exercise, teach your English Cocker Spaniel tricks or engage in new games with it; this will help to keep your English Cocker Spaniel mentally engaged.

4. Stressed English Cocker Spaniels will chew just to relieve some of the tension. An uncomfortable home situation or a new pet or even a new baby can cause stress. Helping your English Cocker Spaniel become used to the new family member can help relieve the chewing problem, and maintaining a calmer atmosphere in the home will also help. English Cocker Spaniels are very sensitive to human moods and behavior.

Hopefully, it is needless to say that physical punishment and shouting have no place in correcting destructive chewing. Reinforce positively when your puppy or dog is chewing something it should. If you catch the animal chewing up the furniture or an article of clothing, pull it away, or remove the object from your English Cocker Spaniel. You can say "No" once to your English Cocker Spaniel, but don't yell or repeat the command. If the problem persists, consider using an animal behaviorist.

Jumping Up

Few people enjoy being jumped upon by their dog or by anybody else's. Children can be knocked over by dogs jumping on them and this can even be a problem for adults depending on the size of the dog. However, it will still be viewed as an annoyance by most people when a dog jumps up on them.

Jumping develops from the English Cocker Spaniel adult or puppy's natural greeting behavior. Dogs greet one another by sniffing the other's face, and when puppies or dogs jump up they are simply trying to do the same thing – get close to our faces. Most of us inadvertently reinforce jumping when the English Cocker Spaniel is a cute puppy and it jumps up to say hello when we have returned from being away.

Almost universally, the usually suggested methods to be used to curb the jumping habit all have a whiff of the Medieval about them: spray the dog in the face with water, step on the dog's feet, knee the dog in the chest, wrestle it to the ground by stepping on its leash, or even hurt the dog's forefeet by squeezing them hard. When you think about it, isn't this just a bit draconian for an English Cocker Spaniel that is just happy to see you?

The most sensible thing of course, is to curb jumping while your English Cocker Spaniel is still a puppy and before the behavior pattern has become ingrained. Preventing jumping behavior will go hand in hand with obedience training. The best approach is to use the "Sit" and "Stay" commands for the puppy when you or anyone else comes into the home. It's also a good idea to train the pup to go to a specific place when you come in, such as next to a chair or on its bed. This will take some time as you are going to have to overcome some instinctive behavior (especially if you have already been allowing your puppy to jump up). Rely on positive reinforcement and treats to help teach your puppy to greet you more calmly and without jumping up. Once the pup is restraining itself, kneel in front of it to let it access your face and greet it affectionately.

You will have to repeat this over and over until your English Cocker Spaniel adult or puppy learns to connect sitting and waiting to be greeted with rewards such as affection and treats. As with other training, repeat the lesson several times over the course of the day, going in and out, to accustom your dog to the new behavior you require. Don't overdo it to the extent that either of you become bored or frustrated.

When you see your English Cocker Spaniel adult or puppy getting ready to jump up onto you, step aside or turn your body so that your English Cocker Spaniel misses. This should be taught in conjunction with the "Sit" and "Stay" commands. If you do come in and your English Cocker Spaniel refrains from jumping, make sure to praise it, even if it isn't in the 'right spot' and isn't sitting. A small step is better than none.

Some measure of success can also be achieved if you use a toy as a distraction. Before your English Cocker Spaniel adult or pup reaches you, offer the toy. This will usually redirect your English Cocker Spaniel's attention from you and prevent jumping.

Territorial Marking

Male English Cocker Spaniels are not the only ones that will engage in territorial marking in the home – females will, too, under specific circumstances. We found that our female English Cocker Spaniels would mark territorially when they first came into the house, and also when they returned from a stay in the veterinary hospital. This was deliberate on their part but was not repeated; they evidently felt the need to either establish or re-establish their presence in the home and we ignored it completely. A one-off marking can likely be totally ignored; it's when the problem is ongoing that steps will have to be taken to curb it.

There are a handful of reasons why English Cocker Spaniels, usually male, will use urine to stake out their territory. A trip to the vet should be taken to rule out any medical problems, but generally, territorial urine marking has other reasons. English Cocker Spaniels that have not been neutered will also be more prone to this problem behavior than those that have been.

1. A worst case scenario is when your English Cocker Spaniel feels that it is the dominant member of the household – the alpha. Male dogs that do this will often keep their human charges in line with growling or nips, so the marking is just a manifestation of a badly out-of-control situation in the first place. Keep in mind that your male English Cocker Spaniel has the same instincts as any other type of dog breed, and it will try to lord it over you if you allow it.

2. English Cocker Spaniels of either gender will often mark when a new pet is introduced into the household, they evidently feel the need to establish themselves as 'top dog' immediately and let the newcomer know its place.

3. A new family member, such as a new baby or spouse, often prompts some territorial marking. Whether this is done to establish peck order or simply from stress is not known, and this usually occurs only once.

4. An English Cocker Spaniel that is under stress or suffering from separation anxiety will be much more likely to mark the home. This kind of marking can be repeated, so finding the underlying cause and addressing it is vital.

Curing territorial marking in the home can be difficult, especially if the English Cocker Spaniel is acting from a position of superiority over the humans. In this case, a way must be found to restore the normal 'pecking order' in the home. This is best done by obedience training, which will help to teach your English Cocker Spaniel how to behave and to respond to your signals. English Cocker Spaniels that persistently urine mark in the home to demonstrate their status over their humans will often also show resource guarding aggression to the humans as well – the dog will growl, snarl, or bark when someone attempts to sit on a couch that the English Cocker Spaniel believes is its personal property.

If the English Cocker Spaniel is not marking to show its superiority, the owner should try to analyze why the animal is doing so, especially if this behavior appears suddenly. Accustoming your English Cocker Spaniel to a new pet or family member can take some time, but most English Cocker Spaniels will come round fairly quickly if they are rewarded with treats and praise when acting appropriately towards the new member.

Clean up the urine immediately to remove a stimulus to future marking. You will need to use not only soap and water, but an enzyme cleaner to remove the odor completely. Enzyme cleaners will break down the organic components that soap cannot. Several applications may be needed before the smell is gone. Never use ammonia or a cleaner that contains ammonia – ammonia is a major component of urine and this will only intensify the attraction.

Keeping a close eye on your English Cocker Spaniel and when it starts to show signs that it's getting ready to urinate, hustle it outside. Once it has urinated appropriately, be sure to positively reinforce this behavior by praising your English Cocker Spaniel and giving it a treat.

English Cocker Spaniels that must be left alone for a part of the day will be more difficult to handle in regards to urine marking. Sometimes this can be done by keeping your English Cocker Spaniel in a particular area; part of a room can be partitioned off, or a crate might be employed. However, any dog will urinate if they are not given the opportunity to do so every few hours, and a dog that has finally urinated after being left alone for 7 or 8 hours is certainly not responsible for this; this is not territorial marking, just desperation. If you are unable to walk your English Cocker Spaniel during the day, please consider having a relative, neighbor, or pet sitter give your English Cocker Spaniel a chance to relieve itself outside.

Punishment for urine marking is never called for and will only serve to make your English Cocker Spaniel fearful and possibly aggressive. Territorial marking can be difficult to correct, and in extreme cases, your veterinarian could prescribe medication to help curb the behavior. A trip to the vet should be one of your first steps, to rule out any medical problems.

10th Chapter: Service and Therapy Dog Training

There is often some confusion about the difference between service (assistance) dogs and therapy dogs. Both types of dog are indispensable in their way, but the goals and training of these dogs differ widely.

Service Dogs

Service dogs used to be referred to as "Seeing Eye Dogs", but their use and training goes far beyond helping just blind people. Today's service dogs perform an extensive range of help to those who are disabled physically or mentally. People confined to wheelchairs, blind or partially blind, epileptic, deaf, suffering from PTSD (post-traumatic stress disorder), and those who rely on medications, such as cardiac patients, all often require the assistance of service dogs to live as normal a life as possible.

Service dogs are not considered to be pets as other dogs are, but are highly trained animals that perform tasks that would be difficult or impossible for their human owners to carry out. These dogs are enabled, by law (in the United States), to accompany their owners wherever they go. The only places a service dog will be denied will be an operating room or anywhere that serious infection might occur, such as a hospital unit that treats burns.

Service dogs are allowed in all public buildings and on all public transportation. It is usually easy to distinguish a service dog since it will be wearing a jacket designating its role, harness with handle, neckerchief, or tag to identify it. These dogs should not be approached – they are working and have been specifically trained to ignore people and other distractions.

It is not uncommon to not only see a service dog guiding a blind person, but these dogs are often seen pulling wheelchairs. Depending on the nature of the disability, some service dogs can remove clothing from the washer and dryer, bring food or medications, alert a deaf owner when someone is at the door or the phone is ringing, or even go shopping.

For those who suffer from epilepsy, their service dog would be trained to alert their human before a seizure occurs, giving them time to get to a place of safety. Epileptics who are stricken in public will be guarded while they are helpless by their service dog (sadly, epileptics who are unguarded have been robbed when suffering a seizure away from their home). Those with hearing problems can use any size of dog – including the smaller dog breeds.

While theoretically any breed of dog, or a mixed-breed, can become a service dog, dogs that have proven to be physically able to perform various tasks while being highly trainable, and good natured, are those best suited for service.

Service Dog Training

Not surprisingly, it takes a good deal of time to adequately train a service dog. In addition to what might be considered 'basic training', dogs must also learn how to perform disability specific tasks, such as pulling a wheelchair, reminding a patient to take medication, or bringing articles of clothing and helping someone get dressed. Not only must the dog master the work needed to aid the disabled person, but it must also learn dozens of commands. The dog must also be comfortable and relaxed around equipment such as wheelchairs or other medical devices. All service dogs are neutered to remove hormonal distractions.

Training a service dog begins when the dog is a puppy, and this is usually done by volunteers who foster the pup. There are various service organizations that help with the training of service dogs and are responsible for placing puppies with their foster families.

Puppies that display a calmer disposition will be more suitable to training than will very energetic ones. A low prey drive is also a prerequisite to becoming a service dog, as aggression is a disqualification for an assistance dog. The training that the puppy will experience at this point will include:

1. Learning to ignore distractions. The puppy will be rewarded with a treat when it does not interact with another person or animal, or resists exploring an object.

2. Obedience training is started. The puppy must learn basic commands including sit, stay, down, come, and heel. The puppy will also learn to respond to direction commands: left, right, stop (wait), forward.

3. The puppy will be taken to a wide variety of situations so that the adult dog will feel comfortable and confident wherever it goes. The volunteers will take the puppy to restaurants, shopping centers, stores, parking lots, hospitals, doctor's offices, and other people's homes. Wherever the pup goes, it must learn to ignore any distractions.

4. Training relies 100% on positive reinforcement, and more intensive (disability-specific training) will only begin when the puppy has reached adulthood.

5. Service dogs often perform complicated tasks, requiring that the dog learn a series of commands in order to complete what is needed – this, too, makes the process of training these dogs a long one.

Puppies will stay with the foster family until they are about a year and a half old, when they will be returned to the service organization for evaluation and more training.

There is a relative shortage of service dogs for those who need them, this shortage, combined with the cost of the dog (often borne at least in part by charitable organizations) means that many people train their service dog themselves, either alone or with the help of friends and family.

Regardless of whether the training is done by a professional or by the disabled person, the goal is to produce a dog that will be capable of reliably filling the needs of the owner.

What might be called 'finishing service training', after the dog has received the preliminary puppy training can take up to 2 years to complete. Dogs that will only be used in the home, for relatively simple tasks associated with deaf persons, can often be trained in a much shorter length of time. The more complicated the tasks that will be necessary for the dog to learn, the longer the training will take.

Until recently, when a service dog became old, and was replaced by a younger dog, the older dog was taken away from the disabled person. However, sanity and compassion has entered the picture, and now the owner is given the option of keeping the older dog, rather than having to surrender it when the new dog enters the home. This has actually been proven to improve the performance of the new dog as it learns from the older animal.

Choosing a Breed for Protection Training

Dogs chosen for protection work must have high intelligence, fast reflexes, courage, and stamina. It would also be ideal for their personalities to be based on a combination of aggression, trainability, and strong bonding instincts. However, owners should be aware that although many of the dogs with these traits will be highly trainable, some could have serious inborn aggression issues.

Always keep in mind that the most important quality you are going to be looking for in a protection dog is the dog's personality. Dogs that have a track record of mindlessly aggressive and untrustworthy behavior will not provide you with the protection you are seeking for yourself or your family; the dog will be just as likely to attack its owner as it would someone who may have stopped at your home to ask directions.

Therapy Dogs

Unlike the service dog, which has to be intensively trained to overcome its instinctive desire to greet other humans, among other things, a therapy dog will be encouraged to interact with people. Few of us can understand the isolation and fear that many people in nursing homes and hospitals feel, comparable to those felt with people confined almost exclusively to the home, due to disability or age, and how much difference a visit from a therapy dog can make.

Therapy dogs are used at disaster sites and in hospices. These dogs are also taken to schools, to help children become familiar with dogs and help them overcome any fears they might have. Not only can dogs help children deal with anxieties, they can also assist in learning how to read, when a child is having difficulty in this area.

Reading to a non-judgmental dog builds confidence and often gets the child started on a lifelong love of reading; the dog is certainly not going to scold the child for mispronouncing a word or stumbling over a sentence.

Therapy dogs can bring some brightness into the lives of people who are living in restricted circumstances. They can also help those suffering from PTSD to overcome their anxiety or panic attacks. It's been proven that therapy dogs actually will cause the brain to release more of our 'feel good' neurotransmitters, endorphins. Not only will these endorphins help to elevate mood, they also will reduce pain levels.

Dogs are not upset or put off by physical or mental disabilities, and it is this accepting quality of therapy dogs that makes them so valuable when it comes to providing comfort and affection to people, regardless of their mental or physical condition.

Unlike service dogs, therapy dogs can be of any breed whatsoever. There are, however, certain qualities that all therapy dogs must have:

1. An affectionate nature.

2. A calm attitude overall.

3. Tolerance of clumsiness, especially in relation to children and older individuals.

4. Ability to ignore jerky movements or sudden, unexpected noises.

5. Not being upset by the presence of another dog.

6. Obeying basic obedience commands.

Dogs used for therapy are usually older dogs as they tend to be calmer to begin with. It goes without saying that dogs with any kind of behavioral issues will not be able to become therapy dogs. Training of these dogs is sometimes done by various organizations or dog clubs, but in many cases, the dog receives training from its owner.

Before a dog can be considered to be a therapy dog, and allowed into different facilities, it will have to be tested and receive certification. There are different organizations that will provide this to show that the dog can be trusted in a variety of circumstances. The American Kennel Club will provide a 'Canine Good Citizen' certificate to show that the dog is reliable, well-trained, friendly, and has a steady, calm disposition.

11th Chapter: The English Cocker Spaniel as a Therapy Dog

People often confuse service dogs with therapy dogs, and while both branches of interaction provide benefits to us, there are some fundamental differences between the two:

1. Service dogs are dogs that are specifically trained to perform tasks that will help a disabled person function more normally. Those who are in wheelchairs, blind, or deaf are those who are most often seen with service dogs. The training of a service dog is a long process as the dog has to learn many different commands and understand how to do a number of different tasks. Training for a service dog begins in puppyhood where the dog first learns to respond to positive conditioning. Obedience training and training for a specific role will follow when the dog has become older; all in all the process can take up to 2 years, depending on the type of service the dog will be providing. We have all seen service dogs guiding a blind person or pulling along someone in a wheelchair, and in general service dogs belong to the larger, stronger, more biddable breeds of dog.

Those who suffer from epilepsy can be warned prior to a seizure by their dog, and if they do have one away from home, their dog can protect them from muggers or other malefactors. Service dogs for deaf people do not necessarily have to be large dogs, a medium sized or small dog will do just as well.

Service dogs are usually easy to identify by the jackets or collars that they wear to demonstrate their status and they are allowed on public transportation and in any public building, even in hospitals, barring operating theaters. Renters cannot be barred from having a service dog in their apartment.

2. Being a therapy dog is a discipline where the English Cocker Spaniel may be able to do well. English Cocker Spaniels have a natural affinity for interaction with people and this can certainly be used to good effect in work as a therapy dog. The training for a therapy dog can actually begin at any age, and nearly any breed of dog can be utilized. Smaller dogs can be ideal because of their portability and ability to be placed right with the target individual. Larger dogs have also been known to do well in this arena.

The purpose of a therapy dog is basically to provide some unconditional affection and emotional support for people who may need these. Although any friendly animal such as a cat, rabbit, guinea pig, or miniature horse can be used as a therapy animal, dogs are the most frequently encountered in this role, due to their trainability and desire to interact with people. While obviously performing an excellent job, therapy dogs are not accorded the same unlimited access to public buildings and transportation as are service dogs.

Therapy dogs have proven themselves to be valuable over and over in a number of different situations. English Cocker Spaniels have been brought to hospitals and nursing homes to bring a bit of spark to an otherwise dreary situation. Many of the inmates in nursing homes will show an uptick in responsiveness after they have had an English Cocker Spaniel sitting on their lap, just happy to see them and giving them some kindly attention. It's not an exaggeration to say that a visit by a therapy English Cocker Spaniel is probably something that people in trying conditions, such as a nursing home, really come to look forward to.

If you are interested in having your English Cocker Spaniel work in therapy, the first thing to do is to make certain that it is completely healthy; the dog should be current on all vaccinations. Rabies vaccinations are required for all therapy English Cocker Spaniels, and other vaccinations might be required by local ordinance; you will have to present proof that your English Cocker Spaniel has received a rabies shot, at the very least, but your veterinarian should be happy to provide you with one. Obedience training is a must for any English Cocker Spaniel (or any dog) that will be used as a therapy dog. Dogs that are used in therapy will be confronted with unusual and sometimes noisy conditions, as well as a number of strange people; an English Cocker Spaniel that is well-trained will be much more likely to take these scenarios in its stride. Needless to say, early socialization is an absolute must for therapy English Cocker Spaniels.

There are several associations that will provide therapy dog training for your English Cocker Spaniel, some of which will provide free training, and others that will require a fee. It is also possible to train your English Cocker Spaniel for therapy work yourself, but it will have to be tested for competence and reliability. Your English Cocker Spaniel must be able to tolerate loud, sudden noises without panicking, numerous people moving around in a strange setting should not bother your English Cocker Spaniel, the sight of another dog (or any other animal) at the facility should be handled calmly, and unfamiliar equipment such as crutches, wheelchairs, gurneys, and IVs with monitors should not startle your English Cocker Spaniel.

Your English Cocker Spaniel should also be able to tolerate handling by people who may have limited mobility or difficulty controlling their movements; the very young and very old will fall into this category.

Once your English Cocker Spaniel has passed the test, you and your dog are ready to begin providing help in a number of ways. English Cocker Spaniels can be led right onto a bed or to an individual without any problem.

1. People in hospitals can easily become depressed, but a visit by a therapy English Cocker Spaniel can help to lift their spirits. Your English Cocker Spaniel will also help to give them something to think about other than their current situation, and can reduce the stress they may be feeling.

2. Cortisol is a hormone released when someone is under stress and is related to a number of detrimental health conditions such as high blood pressure and heart disease. A visit by a therapy dog has been proven to help reduce the level of this stress hormone in the blood resulting in a lowering of blood pressure and a slowing of the heart rate.

3. Therapy English Cocker Spaniels often help to get those who are in nursing homes and hospitals up and moving more. The benefit from a visit by an English Cocker Spaniel lasts longer than the actual visit itself.

4. Basic motor skills also improve when English Cocker Spaniels are available for therapy work. Balance improves quite a bit, meaning that the person will be less likely to fall, and manual dexterity takes a turn to the better as well.

5. Visits to those undergoing treatment is not the only way that therapy English Cocker Spaniels can make a big difference, it's been found that children who are struggling to learn to read do much better when they read to a dog. No English Cocker Spaniel is going to raise a fuss if a child stumbles over a word or hesitates, and the confidence and reading skill of young students who have an English Cocker Spaniel as their audience increases greatly. No English Cocker Spaniel is going to be judgmental or impatient at the way a child is reading.

6. People who are victims of a disaster are often in a stunned mental state, even if they are physically unharmed. A therapy English Cocker Spaniel can help to calm these people down and help them to start sorting out their lives again. Our long

association with dogs means that just being able to come into physical contact with one provides relief from even the most stressful of situations.

7. AAA – Animal-Assisted-Activities – refers to times when your English Cocker Spaniel will be interacting with people who are having extreme difficulties with their motor skills, such as might happen after a serious automobile accident or after surgery. In this kind of therapy, your English Cocker Spaniel will be helping with improving a specific problem, such as helping a patient recover use of his or her hand after an accident or surgery. Undergoing physical therapy can be very stressful, and often painful, but a little help from an English Cocker Spaniel can help the session go more smoothly.

8. Students in high school or in college are often under a terrific amount of stress, especially during exams and tests. Concern about their futures because of a bad test result can really stress these students out, and actually make them perform much worse on the exam than they would have otherwise. Your English Cocker Spaniel can help these students to relax and is certainly a much healthier way to relieve stress than turning to drugs or alcohol.

9. Humans are not the only beneficiaries of the therapy your English Cocker Spaniel provides. It's been found that like the people involved, English Cocker Spaniels benefit from a release of endorphins and other 'feel good' hormones, which help them to be healthier too.

It is perhaps not surprising that the first therapy animal was a little Yorkshire Terrier named Smoky. She helped not only the soldier who adopted her in New Guinea in 1944 when he was ill in the hospital, but she also used the tricks her owner had taught her to help men who were brought in wounded from the battlefield. The doctor in charge of the hospital, Dr. Mayo, was intelligent enough to realize how beneficial Smoky was and let her stay in the hospital.

Your English Cocker Spaniel can now help to carry on the proud tradition that Smoky started by providing therapy to those who need help. If volunteering at a hospice, nursing home, or hospital is too stressful for you, consider those other venues available for therapy dogs.

Bonus Chapter 1: Field Sports Training

While no one can be sure, with absolute certainty, when mankind and dogs began their hunting association, it is thought that our ancestors began to use dogs for this purpose about 20,000 years ago. Dogs appear in hunting scenes from Paleolithic cave paintings, through Ancient Egyptian art, Chinese paintings, and European tapestries and paintings right to the present day. Undoubtedly, the use of dogs increased the ability of early man to obtain food, and was a critical factor in survival.

Specialization of dog breeds probably began several thousand years afterwards, when breeds such as Mastiffs were used to hunt large, dangerous game like lions and boars, and Sight Hounds made themselves useful for finding and running down antelopes and other fleet-footed herbivores.

The development of agriculture and domestication of grazing animals sparked the development of the shepherding breeds, and while hunting for food may not have been as vital as it was before sheep, goats, and cattle were available 'on demand', further refinement of hunting dogs came about over the centuries, resulting in the predominant hunting breeds still in use by today's hunters:

1. Pointers are distinctive by their raised front paw, stillness when pointing, and focused gaze when indicating where game is to be found. These dogs generally course ahead of the human hunter, locating game with their superior sense of smell and then indicating the location by its stance.

One of our English Cocker Spaniel pups, would go on point when she heard a noise outside, which probably goes to show that the hunting and pointing instinct is strong even in dogs that have been intended for and considered to be strictly companions.

2. Retrievers are usually used for hunting ducks and other waterfowl, and are eager not only to bring back the game to their masters, but also plunge into water to do so. These are generally very easy dogs to train, as their hereditary instincts already provide them with nearly all they need to know to carry out their tasks, and they just need a nudge in the right direction to perform as desired.

3. Setters are used in much the same way as are Pointers in that they locate game and then 'set down' before it to not only indicate where the prey is, but also to prevent it escaping before the hunter arrives. Some setters will also point. These are very active and personable dogs.

4. Spaniels are smaller hunting dogs also prized for their pleasant personalities. They are known to be a group of working/ companion dogs that are handy over rough terrain and will not only serve to locate game, and flush it, but will also retrieve. These dogs excel at hunting birds, and in some cases, will happily retrieve from the water.

5. Hounds come in all shapes and sizes and are still used widely for hunting a variety of game, both small and large. Some hounds are often used just as companions rather than for hunting, although their prey instincts are still strong. Rough terrain does not deter hounds on the scent. While it is true that most hounds are not the most trainable of dogs, they do tend to be very good-natured and their natural tendencies for hunting usually just mean that they only need to be encouraged and given the chance to develop their skills.

Hunting dogs tend to be very amiable in their dealings with their human families; hardly surprising considering how long humans and dogs have been working together. Intractable, vicious, or overly aloof dogs would never have worked out as hunting dogs, especially as the dog will generally be interacting with the human family when not on the chase.

Before you do purchase a hunting dog, make certain that you will be able to dedicate enough time to hunting, or otherwise exercising, the dog. Hunting dogs generally have very high energy levels as well as great stamina, and need to be able to use those inborn traits to one degree or another. Those who are not actually going to engage in active hunting should consider training their dog for field sports competitions; this will serve to keep you interacting with your dog, give the dog a feeling of purpose in life, and provide the exercise your hunting breed requires.

In most Western countries, hunting is not generally needed to provide food for the table (although the flesh of birds and mammals is certainly welcome), but is a way to fulfill the hunting instinct present in humans as well as in their dogs. Hunting also reinforces the bond between the two species.

Bonus Chapter 2: Hunting Dog Training: An Overview

Although it may seem obvious that a high energy hunting dog might not be very happy living in a 3 room apartment in a city, some people will acquire very active dogs and expect the animal to adapt to a sedentary life. Most hunting and herding dogs need a good deal of exercise, and a walk in the park after you get home from work will not satisfy this. These dogs often become destructive and develop mental problems if not fully stimulated.

Training a Hunting Dog

Although the dog you choose for your preferred hunting will come to you with some strong hunting instincts, it will be necessary for you to further hone and define these instincts so that you and your dog work together smoothly. When choosing a puppy from a breeder, you want to look for qualities that will be most likely to produce a good hunting dog: friendliness, confidence (not aggression or shyness), strong body, and a good, heavy coat – puppy coats are certainly not going to be as heavy as the adult dog's coat, but you can still get a good idea of how the hair will grow in later on. Don't choose the puppy that comes up and bites your hand, or the one that hides behind the furniture to avoid meeting you. These are indications of a potentially problematic personality.

Remember, too, that your puppy is still just a puppy and you should never expect it to perform perfectly, or not to act up and misbehave to some extent. Most dogs take a year or more to reach adulthood, and if you think back to how you behaved as a child and teenager, it can give you some insight into the behavior of your hunting companion. Patience will be your best friend while training your puppy.

There are a number of basic things that your puppy should learn over the course of its first year with you:

1. Basic obedience. Your puppy should learn all the basic obedience commands: come, sit, stay, and down. The puppy should also be taught how to heel.

2. "Whoa". Most hunters teach this command to their puppy in addition to the basic obedience commands. This command tells the puppy to stop what it is doing immediately and stay in position until the owner reaches it.

3. Crate training. Because your dog will have to be transported, in most cases, to the place where you plan to hunt, familiarizing it with the crate is essential. If you do this sensibly (see our section on Crate Training), your dog will likely travel in its crate to the hunting site without problem.

4. Socializing. You should present your puppy with the opportunity to become socialized with humans and other dogs. This will help to prevent the dog from becoming distracted while on the hunt as well as producing a steadier, more confident dog.

5. Guns. Your puppy will have to become used to the sight of a gun and to the noise. Getting the puppy used to ordinary loud noises around the house will help prepare the pup for gun noise. Also, let your pup get used to seeing a gun before it is discharged (be extremely careful with firearms at all times, especially if you have children in the home). Advice that should be discarded is to shoot a gun off over the puppy's head while it's trying to eat – this might well serve to put the animal off its food altogether and make the pup completely gun-shy.

Another one of our English Cocker Spaniel pups, would become excited and ready to go whenever she saw the rifle or shotgun. If she was inside when she heard the gun go off, she was eager to get out. If outside when the gun was in use, she understood what aiming meant, and after a shot was fired, would run out to see if anything had been hit; all of this without any kind of training for the hunt whatsoever.

You will probably begin training your puppy in the house while it's still very young, and depending on the season, then progress to your yard, and after that to the open fields. Training of the pup will differ according to the type of hunting in which you engage. All hunting dogs, however, will have to learn some commands that will initiate action, such as "Hunt", "Bird", or "Retrieve"; always use the same word when you are spurring your dog to action, using different ones will only confuse the dog and contribute to training failure. Remember that your puppy is a puppy and that puppies will be rambunctious and disobedient at times. Some puppies will, of course, have a strong retrieving instinct and will start bringing objects back to you when only a couple of months old; others may take longer and need more work.

Since their 'invention', training collars, used to deliver a shock to the dog from a distance while being trained, have become popular. This, in my opinion, is completely unnecessary – dogs have been trained over thousands of years without the use of shock collars, and trained very effectively. Hand signals are a much better way to get your dog to respond when it is out of reach of your voice. If you combine the commands used with obedience training with hand signals, it will be second nature to your dog to respond to these signals when in the field. Some hunters use whistles rather than hand signals for this purpose.

Retriever Training

Even if your retriever will be used primarily for upland ground birds such as grouse and pheasants, rather than waterfowl, it's a good idea to get the puppy used to water. Most dogs enjoy swimming or splashing in water, and even dry land hunting could cause your dog to cross a stream in order to bring a bird back. Naturally, confidence in the water will be even more important for dogs that will be used in duck hunting.

Introducing the puppy to water in good weather, a couple of times a week will not only make water familiar, but will also provide the pup with some good exercise. Choose a 'non-threatening' body of water to do this, such as a shallow pond; you might even go in with the puppy yourself if it seems hesitant at first.

Most owners of retrievers use bumpers, or training dummies, to teach their dog to retrieve reliably. These are devices made of rubber or plastic and are evidently derived from the bumpers used to keep boats from scraping against docks. Whatever their origin, they are useful in training your pup to retrieve. Puppies as young as 3 or 4 months can be taught to retrieve using bumpers as long as the training is kept fun and sessions are terminated as soon as the puppy becomes bored.

To use a bumper, the owner need merely give it a toss and encourage the puppy to go after it. Call the pup to you as soon as it has the bumper and praise the animal when it reaches you and surrenders the bumper. You can certainly use treats, but do not use them every time; keep treat dispersal random, but always praise and pet.

Even if you're going to use your dog in waterfowl retrieval primarily, start bumper training on dry ground. Don't start using the bumper in the water until your dog is older and stronger, and choose a warm day to begin water training. The strong instincts of retrievers, combined with bumper training, should make this a fairly easy exercise. You can use a swimming pool, but it's probably better to use a natural body of water (preferably a fairly small one to begin with) during this stage of training.

1. Begin with the puppy in a sit.

2. Throw the bumper into the water and use the command you have chosen, "Retrieve", "Go", or whatever, to get the pup into action.

3. Some puppies may be shy about jumping in and may need encouragement from you. Never shove the puppy into the water. Going into the water a bit yourself will usually help the pup to overcome its apprehension.

4. Once the dog has the bumper, give the "Come" command, which should have the dog heading back to you.

5. The puppy should bring the bumper back to you and release it into your hand.

6. Praise and pet the puppy for a job well done.

Some hunters use the feathers from the kills of previous hunts as an added lure on the bumper. These can be tied onto the bumper and gives the puppy a stronger reinforcement for the type of game it will be retrieving.

As with all facets of dog training, retriever training will take some time, although the amount will vary depending on the personality and inborn instincts of the individual dog, and how much time you are able to devote to it. Some people will leave their pup with a professional trainer rather than train it themselves.

Setter and Pointer Training

Once again, the groundwork for any advanced hunting training will be laid with socialization and obedience and crate training. Training a dog for setting, pointing, or flushing birds will take a fairly long period of time, even if the dog has the most cooperative genes in the world, so be prepared to be patient.

Dogs used in this type of hunting must be taught not only how to quarter a field in search of prey, but to understand what the appropriate prey is. When teaching the dog how to quarter and search, it's best to introduce the puppy to open spaces while it is still very young. Fields that are open, with short grass and few bushes are best at building familiarity with this type of space. As the puppy ages, the fields used can become 'rougher' and more overgrown.

At first, keep the puppy on leash and lead it around the field so that it comes to understand that it is supposed to do this itself. You will have to determine when to let the dog off leash (it absolutely must be obedience trained at this point so that it will come when you call it).

The dog will also have to become accustomed to searching out birds as part of the quartering exercise, and this is usually done with captive birds in cages at different points in the field. Once the dog has gotten close to the bird, help the dog adopt the desired pose and praise it for doing so. Most dogs will understand what they are supposed to do in a very short period of time.

Setters and pointers not only indicate to their human partner where the game is, but are also expected to flush and retrieve it. This is usually done with the aid of dead pigeons. As is the case with most hunting breeds, instinct will certainly come into play early with most puppies, although the exact behavior you seek may take months to achieve. It can sometimes help to have an older, experienced dog work with the puppy – this can make the whole learning process go much more quickly.

Training Hounds

Hounds are usually used for very active hunting, such as hunting rabbits, hares, raccoons, and opossums. These dogs are generally very good-natured, but they all require huge amounts of exercise, and if they are not going to be hunting most of the time, they will need exercise every day to provide what their bodies and minds need. In addition to requiring high levels of exercise, hounds can offer some wonderful challenges during the training process.

As with all hunting dogs, the young hound should be given obedience training and crate training. Always consider that you will have to take more time to teach hounds obedience than you would some of the other hunting breeds, but always keep the instruction positive and upbeat.

Clicker training has been shown to be quite effective when training a hound puppy (please see our section on Clicker Training).

Hounds have a very strong sense of smell and it is this that the owner will use to help train the dog to hunt a particular type of game.

Raccoons are a favorite prey animal in parts of the United States, and these are usually hunted with many Coonhound breeds, and the hunting is conducted mainly at night. When training a Coonhound, the object is to get the dog used to following only the scent of raccoons, otherwise the dog will go after any animal that it detects. Trainers usually begin by dragging the pelt of a raccoon up to a tree and letting the puppy follow this scent to the 'game'.

This lesson will need to be reinforced repeatedly to keep the puppy from becoming distracted, but the natural instincts of the pup and the use of praise should soon help train the animal to follow only the scent of a raccoon reliably. Many trainers follow this up by using a live raccoon in a cage, hiding the cage either in the bush or suspending it in a tree. As with the training provided to pointers and setters, an experienced Coonhound can help the neophyte learn more quickly.

Some of the smaller hunting dogs used to be used in large packs to hunt small game, and although there are still a few places that still do so, most are used singly or in very small groups. These dogs are used mostly to hunt rabbits or hares, and this hunting is done during the day. The object is to have the dog flush out the rabbit then chase it into gun range so that the human hunter can shoot it. Once again, an older, experienced dog is often used to help train the younger one.

Hard Mouth

Part of the work of the retrieving dog is to bring back the fallen bird to its owner in good condition; this is known as having a soft mouth. The opposite, where the bird is returned chewed and bloody, is called hard mouth, and is one of the least desirable traits a field dog can have and one of the hardest to break.

Many trainers believe that the tendency to having a hard mouth is a genetic trait passed down from one generation to the next. Of course, the offspring of soft-mouthed parents could easily turn out to be a complete hard mouth, too.

Besides the genetic factor, there are also other elements that can contribute to this condition, and they can be laid at the feet of the owner.

1. Playing games such as tug-of-war with the puppy just sets the pup up to having a nice strong, hard mouth. Avoid games where the puppy is going to have to really clamp down.

2. In many cases, the mangling of the bird occurs when the dog gets closer to its owner. It is thought that this is because the dog has been stressed out by the owner, and perhaps punished, when bringing game back. The owner may think the dog has taken too long to return, and punishes the dog. He or she is choosing the possible worst time to provide some negative reinforcement – would you want to approach someone if you knew you were going to be punished? Even if the dog has wandered, rather than bringing the game instantly, praise the dog for returning at all.

Although some really awful 'cures' for hard mouth have been suggested, such as having the dog carry barbed wire or wire brushes in its mouth, in most cases there will be nothing that can be done to alter this trait. It's probably best to either accept chewed up birds, or simply get another puppy and start over again, keeping the first dog as a pet and companion.

Precautions

Hunting of any kind is a rigorous activity that can expose dogs to a number of dangers, some obvious, some not so much. It is the duty of the human partner to assure the safety and health of their dog or dogs.

1. Vaccinations. Your dog must be current on all of the required vaccinations, especially rabies, which the dog could contract from rabid wild animals. Heartworm preventive should also be provided to hunting dogs since they will almost certainly be bitten by mosquitoes.

2. Water. Dogs that are used for retrieving wildfowl can become chilled if in the water during cooler weather, but there is another danger to water – water intoxication. Dogs will often lap up too much water while retrieving or swimming and this can cause a potentially fatal upset of the dog's electrolyte balance, and can cause the brain to swell, resulting in coma and death.

3. Ticks. Going through bushes or long grass can certainly expose your dog to ticks. These arachnids can cause serious illness in dogs (our dogs all contracted Ehrlichiosis and Lyme Disease from deer ticks; their treatment cost us over $1,000). Your dog should be examined thoroughly after the hunt for ticks. Deer ticks are very tiny and the males are almost impossible to detect as they are the same size as the period at the end of this sentence. Wood ticks are larger and easier to spot. The sooner you remove the tick, the better. If your dog starts to exhibit pain in its joints, fever,

vomiting, or diarrhea, take it to the veterinarian immediately for treatment; antibiotics will work against these bacterial diseases.

4. Foxtails. Foxtails are the dried seeds of various grasses and other plants. These seeds can make their way into your dog's eyes, ears, nose, and mouth to cause great discomfort. Foxtails can also work their way through your dog's fur into its body, sometimes even drilling into the body cavity. Serious infections have resulted from foxtails. Brush your dog after it's been in the brush to remove any foxtails and pay special attention to the dog's face. Please be aware that foxtails can also embed themselves between your dog's toes and become infected.

5. Burs. Unlike foxtails, burs just stick to the dog's hair and unless removed can cause painful mats and tangles which will have to be cut out.

6. Footpads. Always examine your dog's footpads for cuts or thorns. There are creams and balms designed to toughen a dog's footpads to help prevent damage, and some hunters use boots designed for dogs to protect their dog's feet while on the chase.

7. Cuts and abrasions. Going through rough terrain can cause some wear and tear that your dog will usually ignore while on the hunt. Check your dog over and treat any minor injuries by cleaning them and applying an antibiotic cream – cream works better than ointment as it allows some air to reach the injury to speed healing.

8. Muscle strain. Like human athletes, hunting dogs can also suffer from sprains and strains. Watch for limping when your dog returns from the field; seek veterinary care for any dog that limps.

Proper training and good aftercare can provide the hunter with a valuable hunting partner that will also be a treasured companion, both in the field and in the home.

Bonus Chapter 3: Agility Training

Over the long centuries of the man/dog partnership, dogs have been shaped to serve specific purposes. Dogs have proven themselves to be invaluable in herding flocks of livestock or in hunting. Some dogs have been put to work hauling loads, or acting as guardians of home and hearth. One thing most of these dogs have in common is that they are active dogs that enjoy and need a fairly high level of mental and physical stimulation. These dogs are also very often extremely responsive to obeying commands issued by their master. All of these traits can make some breeds of dog perfect candidates for agility training.

Agility involves you and your dog moving through an obstacle course along a predetermined route, and has become an extremely popular sport. Dogs and their owners are able to demonstrate their prowess in agility at competitions and matches. Success for those who are competing will depend not only on the dog's skill in navigating this course, but also in the time taken to do so. During competitive agility, consideration will be taken as to the dog's size and age, with different categories being assigned.

Many behavioral problems arise in dogs simply because they are not given an outlet for their energy and desire to 'work'. To expect the genetic heritage of hundreds of years to be subjugated so that a specifically conditioned breed will be perfectly happy to lie around the house or apartment all day, doing nothing, is unreasonable and unfair to the dog.

Dogs that destroy their home or yard out of frustration and lack of an outlet for their energy could well wind up in shelters, but very often there is an excellent alternative – agility training. Agility training takes advantage of your dog's intelligence, energy, strength, and desire to work and channels it into something that can be fun for both of you. Working with your English Cocker

Spaniel, as long as patience and positive reinforcement are your guidelines, will also strengthen the bonds between you and your companion.

Agility is a relative newcomer to the dog world, the first beginnings being in 1978 at the Crufts Dog Show in London, and spreading to the United States in 1986. Since then, as the saying goes, 'The rest is history', and now agility is one of the most popular of dog sport activities.

Are All Dogs Not Created Equal?

(At Least as Far as Agility Is Concerned)?

While theoretically any breed of dog can, and probably has, been used in agility training, there are certainly some breeds that will be naturally more successful at it than others.

Keep in mind that not everyone who teaches their English Cocker Spaniel agility is going to do so competitively, and especially as this is still a good way to interact together and have fun. However, if you are thinking of participating competitively in agility, it would be a good idea to concentrate your efforts on mastering the training beforehand.

Those who own mixed-breed dogs can also participate in agility contests, as success in it depends more on the dog's energy level and ability to learn.

Dogs that are always ready to go, responsive to your wishes, and enjoy playing will be the best candidates for agility training. If you have experienced any form of a laid-back attitude, or struggling with training your English Cocker Spaniel, it will be much more difficult to use it in agility.

If this is something that is really important to you, please ensure all of the appropriate training and testing has taken place so that your English Cocker Spaniel will be more likely to fulfill your expectations rather than that which will not. It will spare you from becoming frustrated.

Preparing for Agility Training

Before you begin any aspect of agility training, it is important that your English Cocker Spaniel be reliably trained in obedience. Basic obedience training is what lays the groundwork for the demanding tasks that must be learned if a dog is going to compete successfully. After you have finished with obedience training, it will take up to 9 months for your English Cocker Spaniel to understand what is expected from agility training and to perform as you wish.

Participation in agility competitions is not open to pups under 9 months of age (and very often the dog must be even older) and the cut-off date for dogs is generally 8 years; dogs older than this will not be allowed to compete because they are more likely to be injured.

Once your English Cocker Spaniel has been obedience trained, you can start on agility. If you are hoping to compete successfully in agility, you will need to train your English Cocker Spaniel on the equipment that is used in the obstacle course.

Many people opt to enroll their dog in agility classes, and this has the advantage that you don't have to purchase any of the equipment yourself, although it does have the disadvantage that you must be present at the class in order to take your dog through the agility course and your practice time will have limitations.

If you decide that you do want to handle every aspect of the training, you can set up the obstacles in your backyard. As the routes can vary from trial to trial, the important thing is to get your English Cocker Spaniel used to all the obstacles that could conceivably be used. Get the best equipment you can afford if you are going in for competitive agility (if you are just doing this for fun, you can easily make some of the features yourself). You will need:

1. Teeter-totter or seesaw. Like the child's plaything, this consists of a plank balanced on a stand. The dog will go up the side that is lowered to the ground, then must go to the raised side, and then walk on it to lower that side to the ground. This is the obstacle that will likely present your English Cocker Spaniel with one of its greatest challenges, simply because it is moving. Your English Cocker Spaniel will likely need quite a bit of encouragement and help to master this feature successfully.

2. Tunnels are another feature of agility. There are two kinds used: open and collapsed. The open tunnel is self-explanatory, but the collapsed tunnel has an open entrance that leads to a collapsed cloth tube. The dog must enter and run through both types, and the collapsed tunnel adds a degree of insecurity to the task.

3. A pause table will require that your dog get on the table and then lie down. The dog need only pause on the table for about 5 seconds. The table pause gives the dog a chance to catch its breath for a few seconds and provide a momentary calm.

4. The dog walk is something like a bridge – a plank is raised 4 feet off the ground and is accessed at both ends by other planks. The dog runs up one ramp, across the bridge plank, and down the other side.

5. A marked off square area on the ground, measuring 3 feet on each side, is called the pause box and is used in the same way as is the pause table; the dog must lie down within the box's boundaries for a few seconds.

6. The A-frame consists of two boards, hinged in the middle that requires the dog to run up one side and down the other. Treads are provided to give the dog traction on the boards. The peak of the A-frame is between 5 and 6 feet high.

7. Jumps are an important part of the agility obstacle course and will usually consist of tire jumps, single, double, or triple jumps, broad jumps, and panel jumps.

8. Weave poles are a series of poles, 24 inches apart, through which your English Cocker Spaniel must run, weaving from side to side. Note that your English Cocker Spaniel must always begin the run with the pole on its left side. The number of poles can vary from 5 to 12. Not surprisingly, this will be the most difficult of the obstacles for your English Cocker Spaniel to learn because the movements required for this are not part of the dog's natural 'repertoire'. It can definitely help if you initially arrange the poles as two lines to accustom your English Cocker Spaniel to going between them – gradually moving them together will help your English Cocker Spaniel understand how to maneuver through the poles. To begin with, just let your English Cocker Spaniel walk through the poles; don't try for speed until the poles are lined up correctly and the English Cocker Spaniel has mastered going through them correctly.

Using standardized equipment has the advantage in that your English Cocker Spaniel will already be familiar with the obstacles that will be used in the competition. Some obstacles, such as the crossover, have been done away with as dogs were injured when navigating this. Clubs in the UK still use obstacles that are not used in the United States, such as the sway bridge and swing plank.

Dogs that are hesitant about the teeter-totter, A-frame, or dog walk can often be encouraged by placing a trail of treats on them.

Getting Started

Once you have all the equipment you need (assuming that you are handling the training entirely on your own), it's time to start working with your puppy or dog. When you begin, you will have your English Cocker Spaniel on leash to help it to learn the course reliably. Every time your English Cocker Spaniel goes over or through an obstacle, be sure to treat and praise. The obstacles should be set at the easiest levels to make it simple for your English Cocker Spaniel to become accustomed to them. You can actually set the tire jump and other jumps so that your English Cocker Spaniel can just step over or through them, raising them as your English Cocker Spaniel gains in skill and confidence.

The pause table, A-frame, dog walk, and teeter-totter should all be positioned as close to the ground as possible when you begin. Dogs will have an instinctive fear of heights and most of them will resist going several feet off the ground when training begins.

As you approach any of the obstacles, start trotting and call out the name of the obstacle so that your English Cocker Spaniel becomes familiar with it and associates it with a command. Some dogs may be hesitant or afraid of some of the obstacles when training begins; be patient and rely on treats to help overcome this.

Whatever you do, do not yank on the leash and drag your English Cocker Spaniel through the course – in this case you will probably never have an English Cocker Spaniel that will be able to compete in agility. Stay positive and upbeat; if you seem to be enjoying what you're doing, your English Cocker Spaniel will be more responsive and learn more quickly. The weave poles will take a great deal of practice, especially as the dog will always need to start them on its left side. Naturally, you will not be able to use the leash to guide your English Cocker Spaniel through the tunnels; you will have to rely solely upon encouragement.

When your English Cocker Spaniel has begun to become comfortable with the obstacles, you can start to raise the jumps and tire off the ground. The dog walk and A-frame can also be gradually raised as your English Cocker Spaniel gains confidence. The process of teaching a dog to navigate this obstacle course is going to be a long one, so take it gradually, one step at a time, so that your English Cocker Spaniel can not only become used to the obstacles, but also learn the route of the course.

Remove the leash of your English Cocker Spaniel once it is able to navigate the course without problem. At this point, you will have to rely on your voice and the memory of your English Cocker Spaniel to complete the course. As you will be running the course along with your English Cocker Spaniel, this will make it much easier for it to complete the course successfully.

Competitions

When you decide to undertake agility training with your English Cocker Spaniel, you will likely soon learn that there are two kinds of agility competitions: Matches and Sanctioned Trials. Matches are more informal than Sanctioned Trials and are less likely to have strict protocols. Mongrels are welcomed at Matches, and some of these competitions will even allow you to use food to keep your dog on course, or use a leash. However, for those who are very serious about agility, Sanctioned Trials will be more appealing.

Both types of competitions will require entry fees, with those of Sanctioned Trials having higher fees than Matches. The rules for the competition will be more rigid at a Sanctioned Trial than they will be at a Match. The organizers of the competition will provide the human member of the team with a map showing how the obstacle course will be set up, to allow you and your English Cocker Spaniel time to become used to it.

Joining a club that offers agility classes is also useful for training purposes, even if you have set up your own obstacle course at home, because it gets your English Cocker Spaniel used to performing while surrounded by strange people and dogs.

Sanctioned Trials are held under the aegis of what might be termed 'official' dog clubs, such as the American Kennel Club (AKC) or the Kennel Club in the UK. These agility trials are only open to pure bred dogs; currently mixed-breed dogs are not allowed. Your dog must also be registered with the dog club in order to participate in these agility events. When a litter is born, the breeder must register this with the dog club, but it will be the responsibility of the new owner to register the particular dog with the club.

Dogs entering competitions will be assigned to categories relating to their experience, age, and height. The AKC requires dogs to be 1 ½ years old before being eligible to enter a Sanctioned Trial. Most people who want to enter a Sanctioned Trial will enroll their dog in classes sponsored by the particular club. There are different types of courses that could be used, ranging from Standard Agility through more specialized courses such as Snookers, Jackpot, Teams, and Relay. These latter all offer more challenging obstacles for the dog.

Agility Competition Designations

As it would obviously be completely unrealistic, as well as unfair, to expect dogs to compete with those that might be significantly larger and stronger, or more experienced, most agility trials are divided into classes to make the competition available to all breeds and training levels.

Height is one of the determining factors, with the jumps being set much lower for dogs that measure 12 inches at their withers. Because younger dogs will obviously be less experienced at agility than those that have been practicing for several years, rules for novices will be different, and more flexible, than those for dogs that might be considered masters. Some agility competitions also include older dogs; these dogs are allowed more time to complete the obstacle course and the jump heights will be lowered as well.

Disqualifications

In every competition, there will always be winners and losers, even if the dog does complete the course correctly. There will also be some dogs that become disqualified for various faults. There are quite a few factors that can lead to your English Cocker Spaniel being disqualified during an agility trial. Most of these can be avoided simply by diligent training, but there can also be unforeseen variables that can result in your English Cocker Spaniel being removed from the competition. Depending on the rules set for any Sanctioned Trial or Match, your English Cocker Spaniel could be disqualified for any of the following reasons:

1. Knocking over a bar or panel.

2. Missing a contact (your English Cocker Spaniel does not place its foot in the proper place or exits the obstacle inappropriately – jumps off the dog walk, for example).

3. A time fault results in disqualification when your English Cocker Spaniel has taken longer than the permitted time to complete the course.

4. If the dog runs past the course, it is called a run-out, and is an automatic disqualification.

5. Using food to lure your English Cocker Spaniel through the course.

6. Touching the dog or the obstacles.

7. A dog that eliminates on the course will be disqualified.

8. Refusing the obstacle (hesitation is also a disqualification).

9. Not following the designated course – going off course.

10. Biting the trainer or the judge.

11. Some agility trials not only prohibit the use of a leash, but also a collar; in which case a dog wearing a collar will be disqualified.

12. A dog that starts the weave poles with the right shoulder, or that skips poles will be disqualified.

While there are some agility competitions that offer cash prizes, some of them considerable, most will offer ribbons or perhaps trophies to the dogs that win. The primary reason why agility has become so popular, however, is not for monetary consideration, but for the opportunity to work together with your dog. Agility should be a fun activity for both of you, a way to bond more closely, and an outlet for the high energy level of some dogs.

Dogs that were 'born to work' in one way or another, but that are denied this in the modern world, will often find their instinctive need for physical and mental stimulation adequately supplied by agility training. It should be needless to say, one would hope, that all agility training should be conducted in a positive manner, with treats and praise being the only controls used.

Final Chapter: Closing Thoughts

Positive Reinforcement

Positive reinforcement involves using nothing but praise when your English Cocker Spaniel does something correctly, but ignoring undesirable behavior. This training method is probably the only one that should be used for any kind of basic training: obedience, crate, agility, hunting, etc. Rewarding an English Cocker Spaniel adult or puppy for doing the right thing generally has long lasting results and provides a training structure that the English Cocker Spaniel will be less likely to break.

While this is the most appropriate training method when serious behavior problems are not involved, it will also take longer than the old 'thumbscrew' methods to achieve results. Multiple repetitions will have to be made to teach your pup the correct way to behave, and a good deal of patience and forbearance will be required. However, the results are generally long lasting and will produce a confident English Cocker Spaniel that will be a joy to be around.

Positive reinforcement can also be used to correct what might be considered more 'minor' behavior problems such as soiling the house and barking. These are annoyances and pose no real physical threat to people, so can be dealt with by using patience, praise, and treats. Biting, growling, snarling, and other dominance issues may be too serious, and require immediate correction, to use positive reinforcement exclusively. And, while proponents of positive reinforcement deny that they are trying to be 'pack leaders' or are using any kind of dominance when correcting problem behavior, the fact that the offending dog will be taken to the basement for a period of time, or confined to a crate is showing that the human is the pack leader – he or she is directly controlling the dog's behavior. It is fine that no physical violence was carried out on the dog, but the dog has still been put into a subordinate position where it has to do what the human decides. This is certainly not wrong, but the human has become the pack leader and is telling the underling what to do.

Pack-Leader (Alpha) Training

This has been the basic and most widely used training approach until fairly recently. This system teaches the dog that it is always – always – subordinate to every human being in the house, and has been applied with various levels of correction. On the one hand, according to this theory, you will have some physical correction, such as an alpha roll or slamming the dog to the ground, when the dog has exhibited poor behavior. This is obviously completely inappropriate for house soiling or other non-violent infractions, but is often used when the dog has posed a physical threat to someone in the home.

However, correction collars such as shock collars, choke collars, and prong collars are also not the solution to training, even when there is a serious behavioral problem. Physically punishing a dog is also obviously wrong and abusive, too, and will be more likely to produce more behavioral problems.

Some trainers still use the alpha roll to correct serious behavior problems, but extreme care should always be exercised if you decide to use this yourself. There have been problems such as the dog attacking the person rolling it, or serious damage done to the dog, so any aggression issues should be discussed with your veterinarian. However, as these biting problems usually grow from behavior that was not corrected when the dog was a puppy, the best answer is probably to let the puppy know that growling, snarling, and biting will not be tolerated the first time that the pup exhibits this. A stern "No!" will often be sufficient to let your errant English Cocker Spaniel puppy understand that certain behavior is not allowed; this will not scar the puppy for life.

Many behavior problems arise because the English Cocker Spaniel puppy, and then the adult dog, simply does not understand its position in the household hierarchy. And while early wolf studies were definitely flawed as they were based on captive wolves in a zoo, watching a video or reading about wild wolf behavior will highlight that there are definitely wolves that are in charge and wolves that are not.

The wolves that are not in charge are nipped, growled at, and threatened when they overstep what the pack leaders consider to be their boundaries. Yes, the pack leaders are the parents, but they also are the arbiters of pack life; humans behave this way, too, if they want a peaceful home life – unless an adult rules the roost, family life is chaos. Life in a wolf pack is not a slice of the peaceable kingdom, despite the fiction promulgated in Farley Mowat's book "Never Cry Wolf". Consider that Mowat promulgated that wolves lived almost exclusively on mice and other small game, rather than pulling down deer, moose, and anything else they can get their teeth into, and then ask yourself why this person is considered to be some kind of arbiter of canine behavior.

Some people who believe completely in positive reinforcement object to even using the word "No". I agree it should be avoided as much as possible, but no dog is going to be permanently scarred if its owner says "No" or "Stop" during the training process. Dogs, even English Cocker Spaniels, are rubbery and resilient and will respect and love you more if you and the other household humans are in the alpha position.

Alpha training fell into disrepute for several reasons: some trainers evidently confused training with torture, and trainers promoting positive reinforcement felt it necessary to completely discard the 'old' training method.

A Balanced Approach

Perhaps the best way to approach dog training is to use a combination of positive reinforcement and pack leader training, with a heavy emphasis on the positive. Despite what some trainers now say, it is important for the humans in the household to be at the top of the peck order, and correcting inappropriate behavior in an English Cocker Spaniel puppy, using mostly positive reinforcement for good behavior, but letting the pup know when it has done something very bad, such as biting, with a loud reprimand or even a poke to the shoulder, will often nip this kind of behavior in the bud, before it becomes a real part of the animal's psychological make-up – the longer that problems are allowed to exist, the more difficult they will be to correct. However, never should correction become abuse; if you are unable to correct a problem quickly and without using excessive force, you must seek the help of an animal behaviorist.

Oddly enough, using positive reinforcement exclusively can cause the development of problems just as much as can an emphasis on negative reinforcement; dogs who were subjected to constant negative stress were 25% more likely to become aggressive, but the flip side is that most dogs that received only positive reinforcement developed behavior problems at a higher rate than dogs that received either verbal or physical corrections. In fact, positive reinforcement, when not used in conjunction with some negative, made the dogs more aggressive and fearful – could it be that the dogs felt insecure because there was no real leader? Being in authority does not mean that punishments are distributed constantly, but rather that someone is overseeing (wisely, we hope) the behavior of all individuals in the household and is helping to keep everything on an even keel.

When training your new English Cocker Spaniel puppy, definitely rely on positive reinforcement for most of the process, but combine it with some 'soft' negatives when needed. English Cocker Spaniels are intelligent, and at some level seem to understand that they are not intended to be the leader of a human pack. Submission to the owners does not mean that the English Cocker Spaniel has to cringe and approach the humans on its belly. It just means that the pup knows it can rely on the humans to run the household and that its place is safe and secure.

CPSIA information can be obtained
at www.ICGtesting.com
Printed in the USA
LVHW090058150419
614171LV00001B/69/P